**1904 Cleveland Naps
(preceding page)**

A full decade before they were called the Indians, Cleveland's franchise in the
American League was called the Naps, named for Napoleon Lajoie, the league's
marquee player. Lajoie is seated at center in uniform. Second from left is
Cleveland manager Bill Armour. Third from right is team owner Charles Somers.

INDIANS *Illustrated*

100 Years of Cleveland Indians Photos

by

Mark Stang

ORANGE FRAZER PRESS
Wilmington, Ohio

ISBN: 1–882203–67–4

Copyright © 2000 by Mark M. Stang

Orange Frazer Press, Inc.
Box 214
37 ½ West Main Street
Wilmington, Ohio 45177

Telephone 1.800.852.9332 for price and shipping information
Web Site: www.orangefrazer.com
E-mail address: editor@orangefrazer.com

Library of Congress Cataloging-in-Publication Data

Stang, Mark (Mark Michael)
    Indians Illustrated: 100 years of Cleveland Indians photos / by Mark Stang.
    p. cm.
    Includes index.
    ISBN 1–882203–67–4
    1. Cleveland Indians (Baseball team)–History–20th century. 2. Cleveland Indians (Baseball team)–History–20th century–Pictorial works. I. Title: 100 Years of Cleveland Indians photos. II. Title.

GV875.C7 S83 2000
796.357'64'0977132–dc21

Printed in Canada

For Rosemary,
who makes me better in every way.
— M.S.

Introduction

In the faces on these pages lie the stories, the legends and the lore of Cleveland Indians baseball in the 20th century. Some of the photographs have brief tales to tell; other pictures, as the old saying suggests, are worth a thousand words.

A few of the images are familiar, but I have included dozens of previously unpublished photos and many others that were published only once, long ago. The 240 images in this book, culled from 16 public and private collections are what I believe to be the best available photographs of Indians players though the century.

It is important to note what this book is not. It is not meant to be the 200 greatest players in Cleveland Indians history. It is not meant to be the greatest moments in Indians history, nor a history of baseball in Cleveland. There are, and will be, other books covering these particular topics.

This book is a collection of photos that include the famous, the not so famous, and the long forgotten personalities in Indians history. I chose photos for a variety of reasons. Some players were obvious choices. A book covering 100 years of Cleveland Indians images couldn't very well omit stars like Feller, Doby, Averill and Colavito. But beyond the Hall of Fame caliber players, there are dozens of forgotten personalities whose stories are just as compelling.

When my research uncovered the activities of players like Ray Caldwell, both on and off the field, or the accomplishments of "Duster" Mails, I knew they had to be included. People behind the scenes, the owners and managers, also provided fascinating stories. Woven together as a whole, I sought to paint a picture that did justice to the rich tapestry that has been the tradition of Indians baseball.

I came to see myself as a kind of baseball archeologist, uncovering photographic treasures hidden for decades in dusty old files. The opportunity to bring a long forgotten photo back to life made my search for the finest available images a rewarding one. I hope you will agree.

So I now present to you the obvious and the obscure, the famous and the forgotten personalities of the last hundred years in Cleveland Indians history. As we start a new millennium, I look back with pride on the people and images that have shaped the past century of this city's rich baseball heritage.

Mark Stang
2000

Acknowledgments

This project would not have been possible without the assistance of many individuals. I was given complete access to the photo and clip files at *The Sporting News* in St. Louis, where archivist Steve Gietschier and Jim Meier were their usual helpful selves. Many thanks to Tim Wiles and Pat Kelly (and their staffs) at the National Baseball Library in Cooperstown for their assistance.

Doug Clifton, Bob McCauley and the staff of *The Cleveland Plain Dealer* were gracious enough to allow me access to their photo files. Jan Leach, Susan Kirkman and the photographers of *The Akron Beacon Journal* provided me with dozens of superb images. Librarian Ray Zwick and his staff at *The Cincinnati Enquirer* again provided me the use of their files.

The Cleveland Public Library's photograph collection generated several key photos. My thanks to William Barrow at Cleveland State University for the use of the defunct *Cleveland Press* photo archives. The Western Reserve Historical Society in Cleveland provided one elusive image and the SABR–Ottoson photo collection filled in the gaps.

Professional photographers Doug McWilliams and Ron Kuntz were generous in sharing their work with me. Vintage photograph collectors Dennis Goldstein, Mike Mumby and Bill Loughman willingly shared their treasure troves of ancient images, and their encouragement and friendship spurred me on. Thanks to Ted Patterson for allowing me the use of Tom Manning's scrapbooks.

A deep debt of gratitude is again owed Rosemary Goudreau for her editing of the text. My thanks also to Phil Wood for his thorough fact–checking.

The format used in *Indians Illustrated* owes its inspiration to a 1999 publication I co-authored with Greg Rhodes, *Reds in Black and White: 100 Years of Cincinnati Reds Images*. That book, in turn owes a debt of gratitude to the classic work by Neal and Constance McCabe, *Baseball's Golden Age: The Photographs of Charles Conlon* (published in 1993). Greg did his usual stellar job in layout design on *Indians Illustrated*.

Finally, the behind–the–scenes star of this project was Ryan Asher of Litho-Craft in Cincinnati. His technical wizardry and dedication to providing a quality image is evident on every page. Ryan also executed the cover design.

To all these folks I offer my sincere appreciation for their assistance and cooperation in making this project a reality.

Jimmy McAleer
Manager, 1901

Long before the Cleveland Indians got their start, Cleveland was a major league city but a National League town. The Cleveland Spiders offered fans moments of greatness from pitcher Cy Young and center fielder Jimmy McAleer, considered the most sensational outfielder of his day. McAleer, who owned a haberdasher's shop in Akron, was called "The Loafer" for his seemingly effortless ability to loaf across the outfield and make the most difficult catch. During the 1889 season, McAleer robbed Chicago Hall of Famer Cap Anson of extra bases on a ball hit to the right–center field gap. Anson challenged McAleer saying, "Young fellow, you think you're pretty good." Replied McAleer, "That's nothing. Hit one where I have to run for it."

McAleer first retired in 1898, a year before the Spiders set a dubious major league record that stands today: 20 wins, 134 losses. It was the team's final season in the National League, which the next year reduced the number of teams from 12 to eight.

The move robbed Cleveland, Baltimore, Washington and St. Louis of their major league teams. It also left dozens of unemployed players and several promising territories. And in 1901, Ban Johnson, a former newspaperman turned minor league executive, saw an opportunity to form a rival major league. By offering higher salaries, he encouraged more than 100 National League players to switch to his upstart American League.

McAleer was chosen to manage the new Cleveland franchise, largely because of his marquee name and ability to lure prominent players. After just one season in Cleveland, Johnson asked McAleer to transfer to the St. Louis Browns, where he would manage for eight seasons. McAleer later spent two years as manager of the Washington Senators before buying half interest in the Boston Red Sox in 1912, the year the team won the World Series.

McAleer retired to Youngstown in 1913. Stricken with cancer, he committed suicide in 1931 while listening to a baseball game on the radio. He was 66.

Charles Somers
Owner, 1901–1916

Without the bankroll of Cleveland industrialist Charles Somers, the American League might never have become the first successful challenger to the National League. Using family fortunes earned in the coal business, Somers helped finance four of the league's eight original teams.

When the American League debuted in 1901, Somers owned the new Cleveland Blues, named for the dark blue trim on the uniforms. He co–owned the Philadelphia Athletics with the legendary Connie Mack. He owned the Boston Red Sox the first three years. And he loaned Charles Comiskey the money to establish the Chicago White Sox.

In 1902, to ignite fan interest in Cleveland, Somers spent the money to acquire the new league's premier player, Philadelphia A's second baseman Nap Lajoie. By 1903, the American League had become the equal of the National League.

Based on the American League's success, competitors thought there might be room for a third league. In 1914, the short–lived Federal League was formed and began a bidding war for players. The increased costs of running the team, combined with a downturn in his coal and real estate holdings, left Somers almost $2 million in debt by 1916. League President Ban Johnson, remembering Somers' earlier loans, tried to convince the other owners to return the favor and loan Somers the money to hold onto the team. Johnson was unsuccessful. The banks forced Somers to sell the team to settle his debts. Somers would continue to own the New Orleans Pelicans—the Indians' top farm team—until his death in 1932.

Earl Moore
Pitcher, 1901–1907

Earl Moore threw the first nine–inning no–hitter in American League history. Playing at home on May 9, 1901, he held the Chicago White Sox hitless for nine innings. But in the 10th, he surrendered two runs on two hits and lost the game.

In his first five seasons with Cleveland, Moore won 79 games and, in 1903, led the league with a 1.77 ERA. Two years later, he suffered a terrible setback when his left foot was hit by a batted ball. A newspaper account described the injury this way: "The muscles of Moore's left foot have been torn loose, allowing the in–step bone to fall down and making the pitcher flat–footed." Moore missed the entire 1906 season. He was traded and spent the next two years in the minors at Jersey City. He returned to the majors in 1909 and spent five seasons with the Phillies. In 1910, he won 22 games and led the league in strikeouts.

Earl Moore died in Columbus, Ohio, in 1962 at age 83.

Elmer Flick
Outfielder, 1902–1910

In the spring of 1908, the Detroit Tigers phoned Cleveland to propose a swap of outfielders: veteran Elmer Flick for Ty Cobb, who had just won his first American League batting title at age 21. Cobb fought with everyone teammates, fans and sportswriters—and the Tigers wanted him gone.

Flick had just finished his two best years in the majors, winning the 1905 batting title and, in 1906, leading the league in triples and stolen bases. Flick was the first player to ever lead the league in triples for three consecutive years. He was the first AL player to hit three triples in one game.

Cleveland turned Detroit down flat, a costly mistake. Flick would play just 99 more games before leaving the majors at the end of the 1910 season. Cobb would go on to star with Detroit and become the league's most feared hitter, winning another 11 batting titles over the next 12 seasons.

Flick's early retirement at age 34 was hastened by a mysterious stomach ailment he developed in 1908. A career .315 hitter, Flick was long forgotten by most when, in 1963, the Veterans Committee elected him to the Hall of Fame. He died in 1971 at age 94.

Robert "Dusty" Rhoads
Pitcher, 1903–1909

After two partial seasons in the National League, Dusty Rhoads arrived in Cleveland. The big right–hander paid big dividends in the spring of 1904. The team was in San Antonio for spring training when the two final exhibition games were rained out. Club owner Charles Somers had counted on ticket sales to help pay the team's travel expenses back north. Rhoads had a solution. He asked Somers how much money he needed. Somers said he needed $1,600. Rhoads told him not to worry and left the hotel for the Crystal Palace, the local casino. Rhoads hit the craps table and piled up $1,800 in winnings. He loaned the money to Somers, allowing the team to settle its bills and leave town.

Rhoads' on–field performance was equally impressive. He was a consistent winner for Cleveland. He won 22 games in 1906 and pitched a no–hitter against Boston in 1908, using a pitch he called his "Merry Widow" curve. He added a triple for good measure. Rhoads won 91 games over six–plus seasons for the Naps before pitching three final seasons in the minors with Kansas City, where he was a 20–game winner every year. He retired to Barstow, California, where he worked in the cattle business and was a frequent hunting companion of Ty Cobb.

Napoleon "Larry" Lajoie
Second baseman, 1902–1914
Manager, 1904–1909

Napoleon Lajoie was the American League's first superstar.

He joined the Cleveland Blues in the team's second season. Before he arrived from Philadelphia, Cleveland had a lousy record and failed to draw much of a crowd. The team finished seventh in 1901 and averaged less than 2,000 fans per game. The arrival of Lajoie changed all that. His debut on June 4, 1902, drew a crowd of nearly 10,000 fans and annual attendance more than doubled by year's end.

The fans thought so much of their new star that in 1903, they urged that the team be re-christened the "Naps" in his honor. It was. Lajoie responded to his new surroundings by having two of his greatest offensive seasons. He won consecutive batting titles in 1903–04, and led the league in hits, doubles and RBIs in 1904. Late in the 1904 season, Lajoie was chosen to replace the departed Bill Armour as manager. He would handle the dual roles of player and manager for the next five seasons. The team's best finish would be a close second to Chicago in 1908, when they won 90 games.

Halfway through the 1909 season, Lajoie stepped down as manager to focus on playing. The results were immediate. He had four of his best years at the plate between 1910 and 1913, never batting less than .335. However, after the 1914 season, when he hit just .258, Lajoie, 39, was sold to the Athletics, where he spent his two final seasons as a major league player. At age 42, Lajoie retired with 3,251 career hits. He spent two final seasons as player/manager with Toronto and Indianapolis.

His years after baseball were divided between homes in Cleveland and Florida. In 1937, he was the sixth player inducted into the Hall of Fame. He died in 1959 at age 84.

Bill Bradley
Third baseman, 1901–1910

Bill Bradley, a product of the Cleveland sandlots, spent two seasons with Cap Anson in Chicago before jumping to the upstart American League in 1901 with Cleveland. An exceptional fielder, Bradley was so highly thought of that New York Giants Manager John McGraw tried to lure him away with a three–year contract paying $10,000 a year, more than double what he was making in Cleveland. Bradley opted to continue playing in his hometown. He had a career year in 1902, batting .340 and hitting home runs in four consecutive games at Philadelphia. He also had a 29–game hitting streak, the third–longest in team history.

An attack of typhoid fever during the 1906 season severely affected Bradley's skills. He finished his playing career with two seasons in the Federal League as a player/manager.

Bradley would later spend 25 years as a scout for the Indians. He died in 1954 at age 77.

Bill Bernhard
Pitcher, 1902–1907

In an era when starting pitchers were expected to throw all nine innings, Bill Bernhard was remarkably durable. During his career, Bernhard completed 175 of the 200 games he started. At 6' 1" and 205 pounds, he was an intimidating figure on the mound. The big right–hander came to Cleveland from Philadelphia early in the 1902 season and immediately paid dividends, going 17–5. His best season was 1904, when he went 23–13 for the fourth–place Naps.

After the 1907 season, Bernhard left to manage in the Southern Association, spending three seasons each with Nashville and Memphis. He also managed Salt Lake City for three seasons before retiring after the 1917 season. He died in 1949 at age 78.

Addie Joss
Pitcher, 1902–1910

Addie Joss's remarkable career is remembered more for the tragic way it ended. His nine years in the majors, all with Cleveland, were the stuff of legends.

Joss came to Cleveland at age 21 and in his first game, shut out the Browns in St. Louis, allowing only one hit. Before the year was done, he won 17 games, with a league–leading five shutouts. Tall and lanky at 6'3" and 185 pounds, Joss possessed a blazing fastball and a devastating curveball. His career ERA of 1.88 is the second lowest in the history of the majors. Joss won 20 or more games for four consecutive years, beginning in 1905, including a career high 27 wins in 1907.

His greatest achievement came late in the 1908 season. Cleveland was locked in a duel with the Tigers and the White Sox in the final week of the season. On Oct. 2, 1908, the White Sox threw their star pitcher, spitballer Big Ed Walsh, at Cleveland at League Park. Walsh was brilliant, allowing just four hits and striking out 15. Joss was better. He threw a perfect game. Cleveland won 1–0 and League Park erupted. Addie Joss had thrown the fourth perfect game in major league history. Two seasons later, Joss notched his second no–hitter and seemed destined to rewrite the record books when tragedy struck.

On April 3, 1911, while in Chattanooga for an exhibition game, Joss fainted and was hospitalized. On April 14, Joss died of tubercular meningitis at his home in Toledo. He was 31 years old. His teammates, in Detroit for the Tiger's home opener, announced their plan to go to Toledo for the funeral, forcing the postponement of the game in Detroit. American League President Ban Johnson threatened suspension, but the players held their ground. Johnson backed down and the game was rescheduled. The funeral in Toledo was a huge event, with the Reverend Billy Sunday, a former player turned evangelist, presiding.

Later in the 1911 season, the greatest stars of the American League, including Ty Cobb and Walter Johnson, held a charity exhibition game before 15,000 patrons at League Park and donated the receipts to Joss' widow.

In 1978, the Veterans Committee elected Joss to the Hall of Fame after waiving a clause that required inductees to have played a minimum of 10 years. It is the only time that the rule has been waived.

Harry Bemis
Catcher, 1902–1910

Harry Bemis spent his entire career with
Cleveland. He was small (five–foot–six, 155
pounds) but he was a great defensive catcher. He
hit .255 in his nine years in Cleveland. He spent
five additional seasons back in the minor leagues.

When his playing days ended, he moved to
Worcester, Massachusetts, and worked for the
local telephone company.

Bill Hinchman
Outfielder, 1907–1909

After batting .314 at Columbus in 1906, Hinchman was purchased by
Cleveland for $3,500. He spent three seasons as an everyday player, mostly
in the outfield. He also spent time at several infield positions. After failing
to bat better than .260, he was returned to Columbus, where he spent the
next five seasons. Hinchman got one more shot at the majors. He returned
to the majors with Pittsburgh for four years, but a broken leg ended his
career in 1918.

He later became a scout for the Pirates, a position he held for 37 years
until his death in 1963. He was responsible for discovering stars Arky
Vaughan and Lloyd Waner.

Otto Hess
Pitcher, 1902; 1904–1908

During the 1902 season, Cleveland manager Bill Armour was so desperate for pitching that he persuaded a sportswriter for the *Cleveland Plain Dealer* to advertise for pitchers in his daily column. When Armour arrived at League Park the next day, he was greeted by half a dozen prospective candidates, including 23-year old Otto Hess. Hess caught Armour's eye and was chosen to start the day's game against Washington. The Washington manager, hearing that a rookie was starting for Cleveland, instructed his players to lay down bunts whenever possible. The ploy failed to rattle Hess, who survived ten innings and won, 7–6.

Sent to the minors for more seasoning, Hess returned to Cleveland in 1904. The left-hander was erratic, hitting 20 batters in 1906, still a team record. But he gradually rounded into shape and had a huge year, winning 20 games. It would be the high-water mark of his career. Two years later, Hess would be back in the minors for four seasons before going to the Boston Braves. He spent parts of four years with Boston before calling it quits. In 1926, he died of tuberculosis in an Arizona veterans hospital. He was 47.

Frederick "Cy" Falkenberg
Pitcher, 1908–1913

Cy Falkenberg was a practitioner of the "emory ball," caused by scuffing the ball with a piece of emory board. "All you needed was a spot less than the size of a 25-cent piece to make the ball sink or sail, depending on how you held it," he later remembered.

He perfected his trick pitch enough to win 23 games in 1910 for Cleveland. The following season, he was lured to the newly formed Federal League with a three-year contract at double his Cleveland salary. In 1914, Falkenberg led the outlaw league in innings pitched, strikeouts, shutouts, and compiled a 25–18 record. He would bounce back and forth between the major and minor leagues for the next five seasons before retiring to San Francisco, where he managed a Bay area bowling alley. He died in 1961 at age 80.

Nig Clarke
Catcher, 1905–1910

Jay Justin Clarke caught Addie Joss' perfect game in 1908, but he is best remembered for a home run record of dubious distinction. While with Corsicana of the Class D Texas League in 1902, Clarke hit eight home runs in a single game, an organized baseball record that stands today. However, Clarke, a left–handed pullhitter, played in a park with a right–field fence just 210 feet down the line, at least 100 feet shorter than today's modern parks.

After six seasons with Cleveland, Clarke was traded to the Browns. His career was interrupted by service in the Marines during World War I. At age 38, he returned to play in the minors for another six years. He settled in the Detroit area and went to work for the Ford Motor Company.

Jacob "Bugs" Reisigl
Pitcher, 1911

Jacob Reisigl came to Cleveland for a late-season look after winning 20 games by August for the minor league club in New Haven. On September 20, he pitched the second game of a doubleheader at New York's Hilltop Park. He went seven innings and allowed just five hits, but lost 5–4 in a game shortened by darkness.

Eight days later, in Philadelphia, he threw six innings of relief, but allowed four runs on eight hits and Cleveland lost, 9–3. The season ended days later and so did Reisigl's major-league career. He never pitched in the big leagues again. Reisigl retired to Amsterdam, New York, where he worked for the local power company for 30 years.

Willie Mitchell
Pitcher, 1909–1916

Willie Mitchell was the first pitcher to face Babe Ruth in the major leagues. On July 11, 1914, at Boston's Fenway Park, the 19-year-old Ruth, freshly arrived from Baltimore, was pushed into emergency duty as Boston's starting pitcher. Mitchell struck Ruth out in his first at bat, and later retired him on a line drive to Joe Jackson in left, but lost to Boston, 4–3, with Ruth getting credit for the win.

The rest of Mitchell's career was less dramatic. He spent parts of seven seasons with Cleveland. His best year was 1913, when he went 14–8 with a 1.74 ERA, still the Indians' single-season record for a left-handed pitcher. He was later sold to Detroit for the waiver price and spent parts of three seasons with the Tigers. He served in France during World War I and later pitched in the Pacific Coast League.

James "Deacon" McGuire
Manager, 1909–1911

Prior to his arrival in Cleveland, Deacon McGuire had a long and distinguished career as a catcher in the major leagues. Before the introduction of padded catcher's gloves, it is said that McGuire would routinely put a slab of raw steak inside his mitt to better protect his unusually large hands. Nonetheless, he broke every one of his fingers at least once.

McGuire joined the Cleveland Naps as a coach in 1909 after a brief stint as manager of the Red Sox. He became Naps manager midway through the season after the team's namesake, Nap Lajoie, gave up trying to manage and play at the same time.

Nicknamed "Deacon" for his quiet demeanor, McGuire claimed never to have been fined or ejected from a game. When asked about a questionable umpire's call, he replied, "Even if the umpiring had been bad, I would not have said a word." The soft approach failed to pay dividends. He never had a winning record anywhere he managed. Early in the 1911 season, McGuire was replaced by the more popular George Stovall. McGuire spent the next 12 years as a scout for the Tigers.

Terry Turner
Infielder, 1904–1918

Terry Turner stole 254 bases during his 15 years with Cleveland, the Indians team record until broken by Kenny Lofton in 1996. After suffering repeated ankle injuries from sliding, Turner is credited with introducing the head-first slide to the majors. "I suppose head-first slides were dangerous, too, for I still have scars on my hands where I was stepped on," he later recalled.

Turner was a light-hitting defensive specialist, who 10 times led the American League in fielding for a third baseman. He retired after the 1920 season and worked as a superintendent for the Cleveland Street Department until 1952.

Ted Easterly
Catcher, 1909–1912

A catcher who hit for a high average, Ted Easterly was often used as a pinch hitter. Cleveland signed Easterly after he spent just one season in the Pacific Coast League. Midway through the 1912 season, he was sold to the White Sox to make room for Steve O'Neill. In 1914, Easterly followed his former Cleveland manager, George Stovall, to the Federal League. In retirement, he worked as a carpenter before his death in 1951.

George Stovall
First baseman, 1904–1911
Manager, 1911

George Stovall was a player of average ability with a fiery temper. During the 1907 season, Stovall hit player–manager Nap Lajoie over the head with a chair for bumping him down in the batting order. But he was enormously popular with his teammates and when "Deacon" McGuire was fired three weeks into the 1911 season, Stovall was the unanimous choice to take over managing the Naps.

His aggressive style pushed the team from last place to third by season's end. Nevertheless, Stovall was traded to the St. Louis Browns in the offseason, succeeding Bobby Wallace as manager in the last half of the 1912 season.

His temper got him in trouble again in St. Louis in 1913. While vehemently disputing a call by umpire Charley Ferguson, he spit on Ferguson's coat, which led to a 10–game suspension. Later that year, with the Browns in last place, he was fired and replaced by a young Branch Rickey, who would go on to fame with the cross–town Cardinals. In 1914, Stovall was among the first group of players who jumped to the newly formed Federal League.

Neal Ball
Infielder, 1909–1912

Neal Ball produced the major league's first unassisted triple play. It happened on July 19, 1909, at League Park. Cy Young was on the mound and the runners were advancing on a 3–2 count. Red Sox hitter Amby McConnell hit a line drive to Ball, who made the catch, stepped on second to double off base–runner Heinie Wagner, then ran down advancing base–runner Jake Stahl between first and second base to complete the trifecta. Ball would later add an inside–the–park home run for good measure in the Naps' 6–1 victory.

In 1952, a family friend helped Ball retrieve his glove from a trunk in the attic and send it to the Hall of Fame in Cooperstown.

Denton "Cy" Young
Pitcher, 1909–1911

Denton True "Cy" Young spent his first nine major-league seasons in Cleveland. At age 42, he came back for a second time. Along the way, he put up amazing numbers. He won 20 or more games in 16 seasons. In five of those years, he won more than 30 qames.

Young started his career with the Cleveland Spiders in 1890. When Spiders owner Frank Robison transferred the team's best players to his St. Louis franchise, which he also owned, Young went too and won 46 games in two seasons.

The game's marquee pitcher, Young was lured to the newly formed American League in 1901. He spent eight years with the Boston Red Sox and amassed 193 victories. Young notched two wins in the first World Series in 1903, throwing three complete games in his only post-season appearance.

Young returned to Cleveland in 1909 and won 19 games. The following season, he recorded his 500th victory on the way to a career total of 511 wins, a mark that should remain unchallenged for the ages. His 7,356 innings pitched is also first on baseball's all-time list. In 1937, Cy Young was elected to the Hall of Fame.

Napoleon Lajoie
1910 World Series, Shibe Park

With the Naps stuck in fifth place as the 1910 season wound to a close, the race for the American League's batting crown took center stage. Detroit's Ty Cobb, winner of three straight titles, and Cleveland's Napoleon Lajoie were percentage points apart in the final week of the season. The winner stood to win a new Chalmers 30 touring car.

Cobb, despised by players around the league, sat out the final two games of the season, believing he had won with a .385 average. Lajoie, in St. Louis for a double–header on the final day of the season, was a beloved figure. After Lajoie blasted a triple in his first at bat, Browns Manager Jack O'Connor ordered his third baseman to drop back and, suspiciously, to stay back. Lajoie proceeded to drop down six straight bunts for base hits. His seventh at bat resulted in a fielder's choice and his eighth and final at bat was a grounder to Browns shortstop Bobby Wallace, whose wild throw to first was scored as a hit for Lajoie.

Lajoie's eight hits in eight official at bats looked fishy to almost all observers, including American League President Ban Johnson. He summoned the involved parties to his office in Chicago and after hearing the players' testimony, ordered Browns manager O'Connor fired. It was also discovered that the official scorer had been promised a free suit of clothes if he gave Lajoie any close calls at first. It wasn't enough. The final tally placed Cobb at .385, just a single point ahead of Lajoie's .384. In the end, the Chalmers company decided to award autos to both players.

In 1981, researchers for *The Sporting News* reconstructed the 1910 season for Cobb and Lajoie. They discovered that Cobb had two hits mistakenly counted twice and two hitless at–bats never included, thus reducing his season average from .385 to .382. Lajoie also had one hitless at–bat overlooked, reducing his average from .384 to .383. When presented with the evidence, Commissioner Bowie Kuhn refused to have the record books changed.

"Shoeless" Joe Jackson
Outfielder, 1910–1915

Joe Jackson's debut in the major leagues failed to foreshadow his greatness. After two very brief trials with Connie Mack's Philadelphia Athletics, Jackson found himself back in the minors with New Orleans. When the Athletics needed an additional outfielder, they traded Jackson to Cleveland for Briscoe Lord. Jackson, still in New Orleans, responded by hitting .354. and was called to Cleveland for the final month of the 1910 season. In the final 20 games, Jackson finally showed his potential by hitting .387.

During his first full season in Cleveland, Jackson hit .408. He followed with seasons of .395, .373 and .338. He led the league in triples in 1912; and in hits and doubles in 1913. His smooth swing and strong arm made him the idol of school boys nationwide. However, Cleveland owner Charles Somers' mounting financial problems forced him to sell Jackson to the Chicago White Sox for $31,500 and three mediocre players. No one will ever know what Jackson's final career stats might have been had he stayed in Cleveland. The "Black Sox" betting scandal of 1919 brought a premature end to Joe's career.

Napoleon Lajoie Day
League Park, 1912

On June 4, 1912, prior to a game at League Park, local hero Napoleon Lajoie was presented with a nine–foot–high floral horseshoe festooned with more than 1,000 silver dollar pieces. It was a gift from his adoring fans.

Sylveanus "Vean" Gregg
Pitcher, 1911–1914

Vean Gregg overpowered the Pacific Coast League in 1910. Pitching for Portland, Gregg won 32 games, threw 14 shutouts and struck out 376 batters in 320 innings. His left-handed delivery proved equally baffling to American League hitters. With Cleveland in 1911, he compiled a 23–7 record and led the league with a 1.81 ERA. Each of the next two seasons, he produced identical 20–13 records.

When asked by reporters the secret of his success, Gregg, a plasterer in the off season, commented, "I use the same grip on the ball that I used on the trowel." A sore arm in the spring of 1914 led to a trade to the Red Sox. Gregg would bounce between the major and minor leagues for several years, twice winning 20-plus games for Providence and Seattle, before retiring to try his hand at dairy farming in Canada. In 1925, at age 40, he was lured out of retirement by Washington and helped pitch them to the pennant. He died in 1964 at age 79.

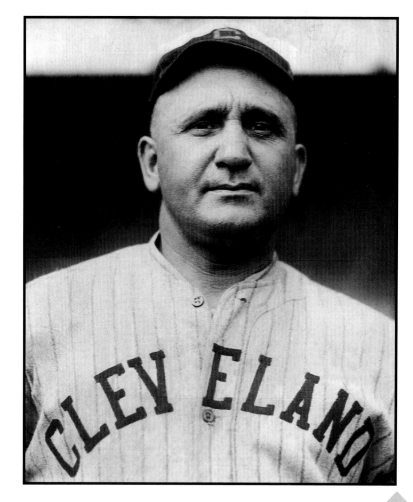

Lee Fohl
Manager, 1915–1919

Lee Fohl was considered manager material because he won several minor league pennants before joining the Indians as a coach in 1915. When Manager Joe Birmingham was released in May, Fohl was named to replace him. Fohl took a seventh-place club and improved it each year, finishing second in 1918.

However, on July 18, 1919, with the Indians having recently slipped from first place to third, Fohl's fortunes changed when the Boston Red Sox came to town. In the ninth inning, with the Indians holding a 7–4 lead, Babe Ruth came to the plate with the bases loaded. Fohl brought in left-handed pitcher Fritz Coumbe to face the left-handed hitting Ruth. The move backfired. Ruth hit the second pitch high over the right-field wall and won the game, 8–7. Indians owner Jim Dunn summoned Fohl to his office after the game and fired him on the spot. He replaced him with his popular center fielder, Tris Speaker.

Fohl would later manage the Browns and Red Sox for three years each during the 1920s. He later ended up managing a gas station in Cleveland for many years before his death in 1965.

Charles "Chick" Gandil
First baseman, 1916

"Chick" Gandil played first base for the Washington Nationals for four years. But once Washington owner Clark Griffith started fining him $10 every time he caught him smoking between innings, Gandil demanded a trade. The Indians gladly paid $7,500 to bring Gandil to Cleveland. But within a year, he was dealt to the White Sox with a foot injury and a slumping bat.

Gandil's lasting fame would come as ringleader of the infamous eight Sox players who conspired to throw the 1919 World Series. He was already out of the majors when he was suspended for life—along with Joe Jackson and six others—by Commissioner Kennesaw Mountain Landis following the 1920 season. Gandil drifted to California, where he worked as a plumber before dying in obscurity in 1970.

Robert "Braggo" Roth
Outfielder, 1915–1918

Braggo Roth was one of three players who came to Cleveland when the Indians traded "Shoeless Joe" Jackson to the White Sox in 1915. Roth's seven home runs led the American League in 1915, an era when home runs were hard to come by. It's called the "dead ball" era because the same baseball was used all game long. Roth was exceptionally quick. In 1917, he stole home six times and other bases 45 times. Roth played for six different teams in his eight-year career. He was killed in a car accident in Chicago in 1936.

In this photograph, you can see Roth's uniform number on the left sleeve. The Indians were the first team in the majors to experiment with uniform numbers, using them briefly in 1916 and 1917 on the sleeves of their home jerseys. In 1929, the club permanently added numbers to the backs of their players' jerseys.

Jack Graney
Outfielder, 1908; 1910–1922

Jack Graney could claim some famous firsts. He was the first batter to face a 19–year–old pitcher named Babe Ruth in 1914. And during his first spring training as a pitcher, Graney's first pitch hit team manager Nap Lajoie in the head. Later that night, Lajoie told Graney, "All wild men belong out west, so I'm sending you to Portland."

Two years later, Graney, now an outfielder, returned to Cleveland for good and spent the next 13 seasons patrolling left field at League Park. Nicknamed "Wait 'em out Jack" for his keen batting eye, Graney twice led the league in walks. He also gained fame for his dog, Larry, who served as the team's mascot and accompanied the team on road trips.

After retiring from the game, Graney ran a Cleveland car dealership for 10 years. But in 1932, he returned to the ballpark for one more first. Graney came back to broadcast Indians' games on WHK, where he would win a whole new generation of fans over the next 22 seasons. Graney is believed to be the first former player to make the transition to broadcasting. He died in 1978 at age 91.

Tris Speaker
Center fielder, 1916–1926
Manager, 1919–1926

Like Napoleon Lajoie 14 years earlier, Tris Speaker was a superstar when he was sold to Cleveland in April 1916.

Speaker played in two World Series, was the 1912 American League MVP and was considered the finest center fielder in the game. But in 1916, Boston Red Sox owner Joseph Lanin refused Speaker's demand for a raise—from $9,000 to $15,000. Lanin told the newspapers that he would trade Speaker before giving in to his demands.

A Cleveland sportswriter saw the story on the news wire, contacted the Indians' owners and suggested they make an offer for Speaker. Several phone calls later, the deal was done. Speaker came to Cleveland for $55,000 and two players. While Lanin thought he had won, there was one catch. Speaker refused to join the Indians unless he received $10,000 of the purchase price—and the money had to come from Lanin, personally. With the season scheduled to open the next day at League Park, Speaker refused to suit up until assured by AL president Ban Johnson that Lanin, and no one else, would pay the bonus.

His first year in Cleveland, Speaker had a career year. He led the league in hits and doubles, and won the batting title with a .386 average. The fans of Cleveland had a new hero.

"Sunny Jim" Dunn
Owner, 1916–1922

When Indians' owner Charles Somers found himself $1.8 million in debt in 1916, bankers forced him to sell the ball club to settle his debts. American League President Ban Johnson found a group of Chicago businessmen eager to purchase the club. The group was headed by Jim Dunn, who owned a railroad construction firm. With a loan from White Sox owner Charles Comiskey, Dunn and the others raised the $500,000 to buy the team.

Nicknamed "Sunny Jim" for his smiling disposition, Dunn gave Indians' fans new hope. His acquisition of Tris Speaker just days before the start of the 1916 season put Cleveland back on the baseball map. His deep pockets helped mold a club that four years later, in 1920, brought Cleveland its first World Championship. As was the custom of the day, Dunn re–named League Park "Dunn Field" in his own honor. He died in Chicago in 1922 at age 56.

George Dickerson
Pitcher, 1916

That there is even a photograph of George Dickerson wearing a Cleveland uniform is a minor miracle. His entire major league pitching career consisted of one inning of relief in 1916. On August 2, 1916, Dickerson entered the eighth inning of a game in Philadelphia with the Indians trailing, 5–1. He held the Athletics hitless, but the Indians still lost, 5–4. Dickerson never pitched in the major leagues again. In 1938, he died in a veteran's administration hospital in Los Angeles. He was 46.

Otis Lambeth
Pitcher, 1916–1918

Cleveland purchased Otis Lambeth for $4,750 after he pitched a no–hitter for Topeka in 1916. Before World War I intervened, Lambeth's sidearm delivery produced 11 wins over two–plus seasons. Lambeth served in France with an artillery battalion. After he returned, he spent time in the minor leagues before returning to his native Kansas. He spent the next 26 years working for the post office.

Spring Training
New Orleans, 1917

Long before ballplayers lifted weights, players in 1917 passed a heavy medicine ball, back and forth, to stay in shape. Caught in mid-session are, clockwise from ball, pitcher Ed Klepfer, scout Jack McCallister, outfielder Milo Allison, pitcher Stan Coveleski, outfielder Joe Wood, first baseman Lou Guisto, pitcher Clarence "Pop Boy" Smith, infielder Ivon Howard and pitcher Guy Morton, who is passing the ball.

Doc Johnston
First baseman, 1912–1914; 1918–1921

Wheeler Roger Johnston spent seven seasons with Cleveland, five as the starting first baseman. He and his brother Jimmy were the first brothers to face each other in a World Series—in 1920, when Jimmy was Brooklyn's third baseman. A lifetime .263 hitter, Johnston's best season was 1919 when he hit .305. After the 1921 season, he was sold to the Athletics. A year later, he went to the minors where he spent seven years playing and managing. He retired to his native Chattanooga and worked in the fuel oil business until his death in 1961 at age 73.

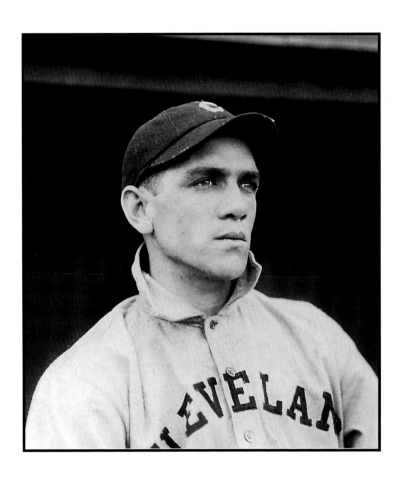

Steve O'Neill
Catcher, 1911–1923
Manager, 1935–1937

Steve O'Neill, one of 13 children born to Irish immigrants, quit school at age 12 to work in the coal mines of northeast Pennsylvania. His brother, the manager of the minor-league club in Elmira, invited him for a visit and wound up putting him behind the plate because the team's two regular catchers were hurt. He never went back to mining coal.

O'Neill played two seasons in the minors before being brought to Cleveland at age 20. By 1915 he was the Indians' everyday catcher. Slow of foot but with a talent for blocking base runners from the plate, O'Neill caught all seven games of the 1920 World Series and batted .300. He was traded to the Red Sox prior to the 1924 season and finished his career with the St. Louis Browns.

In 1929, O'Neill began a career as a player/manager in the minor leagues. In 1935, he returned to Cleveland as a coach. When Manager Walter Johnson was released in mid-season, O'Neill was named his replacement. Considered a player-friendly manager, O'Neill managed no better than a fourth-place finish in 1937 and was replaced by Oscar Vitt. He would later manage the Tigers, Red Sox and Phillies, and win the 1945 World Series with Detroit. Steve O'Neill never had a losing season in his 14 years as a major-league manager. He died of a heart attack in Cleveland in 1962 at age 69.

Joe Evans
Infielder/outfielder, 1915–1922

Despite batting .308 in the 1920 World Series, Evans was only a part-time player during his eight years in Cleveland. He was traded to Washington in 1923 and to St. Louis two years later. While playing for the Browns, Evans attended medical school. He retired from baseball to return to Mississippi, where he practiced medicine for 25 years until his death in 1953.

Elmer Smith
Outfielder, 1914–1921

Elmer Smith is best remembered for hitting the first grand–slam home run in World Series history. In Game 5, with the 1920 Series knotted at two games apiece, Smith faced Brooklyn spitballer Burleigh Grimes in the first inning. Grimes got two strikes on him before wasting two pitches out of the strike zone. After a short conference with his catcher, Grimes challenged Smith with a fastball. The result: Smith drove the ball over the right field wall, propelling the Indians to an 8–1 victory. Unfortunately, Smith's feat was overshadowed by Bill Wambsganss' unassisted triple play in the fifth inning.

Smith had a career year for the Indians in 1920, batting .316 with 103 RBIs. He later spent time with the Red Sox, Yankees and Reds, before putting in seven more years in the minors. He led the Pacific Coast League in home runs in 1926 and again in 1927. Smith later returned to Cleveland and spent ten years as a salesman for the Leisy Brewing Company. He died in 1984 at age 91.

Guy Morton
Pitcher, 1914–1924

Guy Morton was a tall right–hander with an overpowering curveball. When he threw a no–hitter for Waterbury, CT., in 1914, Cleveland promoted him to the majors. Morton proceeded to lose his first 13 decisions, a major league record for consecutive losses at the start of a career. Morton held the record until 1982, when Minnesota Twins pitcher Terry Felton lost his first and only 16 decisions.

Reflecting on his horrible start, Morton later recalled, "You see, I was troubled by what I guess they call stage fright. I used to get nervous and couldn't seem to get the ball to break right." In 1915, he found his groove, throwing two one–hit games and compiling 16 wins. On June 11, 1916, he struck out 13 Athletics. Released by the Indians during the 1924 season, Morton spent eight years pitching in the minor leagues. He died of a heart attack in 1934 at age 40.

Stanley Coveleski
Pitcher 1916–1924

Born Stanislaus Kowalewski to Polish immigrant parents, Coveleski left school after the fourth grade to work in the coal fields of eastern Pennsylvania. The youngest of five brothers, three of whom made it to the major leagues, he spent eight seasons in the minors before joining Cleveland in 1916. While with Portland in the Pacific Coast League, he learned a new pitch, the spitball. "I had as good control over the spitball as I had on my fastball. There was an art to throwing a good spitter. One thing you needed was a jaw full of slippery elm. Went to my mouth every pitch. I'd go maybe two or three innings without throwing a spitter, but I'd always have them looking for it."

In his second season with Cleveland, Coveleski won 19 games and led the league with nine shutouts. Starting in 1918, he won more than 20 games for four straight years. Although he won 172 games in nine seasons, Cleveland sent Coveleski to Washington in 1925, believing him past his prime. He proved the Indians wrong by winning 13 straight games, posting a 20–5 record and leading the league with a 2.84 ERA. After three years with the Senators, he spent one final season with the Yankees. He retired to run a service station in South Bend, Indiana, after the 1928 season. Coveleski was elected to the Hall of Fame in 1969.

Joe Wood
Outfielder, 1917–1922

Joe Wood's career is a story with two distinct chapters. Originally dubbed "Smoky Joe" for his blazing fastball, Wood is considered one of the fastest pitchers ever to play in the major leagues. In 1911, he won 23 games for the Boston Red Sox, including a no–hitter against the Browns. The next year was even more sensational. Wood won 34 games, threw 10 shutouts and completed 35 of the 38 games he started. In that fall's World Series, he won three games and helped the Red Sox defeat the New York Giants in seven games. At 23, Wood appeared headed for greatness.

But in the spring of 1913, he slipped while fielding a grounder and broke the thumb on his pitching hand. He would never again win more than 15 games in a season. He spent the 1916 season at home on his farm because the pain in his shoulder failed to respond to treatment. His career appeared over at 26.

Always a good hitter, Wood called up his former Red Sox roommate, Tris Speaker, in Cleveland, and begged for a second chance. Speaker convinced Indians Manager Lee Fohl to take a chance on Wood. Purchased for $15,000 in 1917, Wood joined his old friend in spring training in New Orleans as a pitcher. The next year, with a war–time shortage of players, Wood was pressed into service as an outfielder. He saw part–time duty over the next five seasons, but appeared in four games during the 1920 World Series. After the 1922 season, Wood accepted an offer to be the baseball coach at Yale, where he spent 20 years before retiring in 1942.

Bill Wambsganss
Second baseman, 1914–1923

The son a Lutheran minister, "Wamby" chose a career in baseball rather than follow in his father's footsteps. A light–hitting infielder, Wambsganss is best remembered for turning an unassisted triple play in Game 5 of the 1920 World Series.

With Brooklyn runners at first and second, pinch–hitter Clarence Mitchell lined the ball straight to Wambsganss, who caught it then stepped on second base to double off Brooklyn base–runner Pete Kilduff. He then tagged the charging base–runner, catcher Otto Miller, who mistakenly believed the ball had made it through to the outfield. Wambsganss was modest about his feat, saying, "Of course it was just luck. Somebody, someday, who happens to be in just the right spot, will do it again." Eighty years later, no one has. At least not in the World Series.

Wambsganss was traded after the 1923 season. He retired to Lakewood, Ohio, and worked as a salesman for a hardware manufacturer. In the 1940s, Wambsganss managed the Muskegon and Fort Wayne teams in the All–American Girls Baseball League. He died in 1985 at age 91.

Ray Chapman
Shortstop, 1912–1920

At age 29, Ray Chapman had everything going for him. He was immensely popular after eight years as the Indians' shortstop. The team was in first place. His wife Kathleen was expecting and they were set to move into a new house.

A single pitch changed everything.

On the afternoon of August 16, 1920, the Indians were playing the Yankees at the Polo Grounds in New York. The Yankees' starting pitcher was Carl Mays, a "submarine" pitcher with an unorthodox delivery. In the top of the fifth inning, Chapman, who crowded the plate, came to bat. Mays' first pitch came in high and tight. Chapman froze. The ball struck Chapman near the left temple, dropping him to the ground. He got up, took one step toward first base and collapsed. He was taken to a nearby hospital, but died the next morning. He is the only major league player to die from injuries received on the field of play.

Four days later, all of Cleveland turned out for Chapman's funeral. Thousands mobbed St. John's Cathedral in a service presided over by 24 priests. A local newspaper collected donations from 20,000 mourners and bought a floral arrangement over nine feet long and six feet wide. Indians Manager Tris Speaker was so distraught that he didn't attend the service. The entire team wore black armbands for the remainder of the 1920 season.

Tris Speaker
Player/manager, 1919–1926

Tris Speaker was reluctant to become manager when Indians owner Jim Dunn fired Lee Fohl in July 1919. He didn't want to be seen as pushing Fohl out the door. But once the star center fielder took over, the team went 39–21 and ended the season just 3½ games behind the White Sox.

Speaker proved a great judge of talent. He promoted pitcher George Uhle, signed pitcher Ray Caldwell and set the stage for the team's success in 1920. He juggled the line–up, platooned players and in the aftermath of Ray Chapman's death, campaigned to make 21–year–old Joe Sewell, playing in New Orleans, the new shortstop. He found Walter "Duster" Mails pitching in Sacramento and convinced Dunn to spend $10,000 to secure him for the stretch drive. Led by his own .388 average, everything jelled under Speaker to bring Cleveland their first championship of the 20th century.

Speaker managed for another six seasons and led the Indians to second–place finishes in 1921 and 1926. After playing two final seasons for the Senators and Athletics, Speaker retired with 3,515 career hits and a lifetime .344 batting average. He later returned to Cleveland as a broadcaster and coach. He was elected to the Hall of Fame in 1937.

Jim Bagby, Sr.
Pitcher, 1916–1922

Jim Bagby's best pitch was the "fadeaway." With it, he won 23 games in 1917, including eight shutouts. In the 1920 championship season, he won 31 games and led the league in innings pitched and complete games. In Game 5 of the 1920 World Series, he added a home run, the first ever hit by a pitcher in the Series.

After winning 118 games in six seasons, the toll began to show on the tall Georgian. He was traded to Pittsburgh after winning just four games in 1922. At age 36, Bagby was finished in the majors. He pitched in the minor leagues for another six years before retiring in 1929 to operate a dry cleaning store and gas station in Atlanta. In 1941, he briefly returned to the minors as an umpire, but suffered a stroke during a game. He died in 1954 at age 64.

Larry Gardner
Third baseman, 1919–1924

Larry Gardner won three World Series titles in Boston before joining his old teammate, Tris Speaker, in Cleveland. In a trade that would pay big dividends, the Indians sent Braggo Roth to the Athletics for Gardner and Charlie Jamieson, both key players on the 1920 championship team. An excellent defensive third baseman, Gardner would hit over .300 five times in the majors.

Hitting great Ty Cobb, not one for lavishing praise, later proclaimed, "Larry Gardner was the best third baseman I ever played against." For his part, Gardner said Cobb never attempted a bunt against him "because I found out his secret early. Cobb used to fake a lot of bunts, but I noticed that when he was really going to bunt, he (Cobb) always licked his lips. When I saw that, I'd start in with the pitch. He never realized I'd caught on."

Gardner was released after the 1924 season and spent three years in the minors. He then returned to his native Vermont, where he spent the next 20 years as baseball coach and, later, athletic director for the University of Vermont. He died in 1976 at age 89.

Walter "Duster" Mails
Pitcher, 1920–1922

John Walter Mails was a pitcher and a showman who joined the Indians late in the 1920 season. He went 7–0 in eight starts and helped propel the Indians into the World Series. There, he held Brooklyn scoreless for 15⅔ innings in two appearances. Mails won Game Six on a three-hit shutout. The next year, he went 14–8 for Cleveland.

Throughout his career, Mails bounced between the major and minor leagues but was a huge gate attraction everywhere he pitched. He drove a car with "The Great Mails" painted on the side to advertise the days he pitched. He offered autographed photos to any woman who would bake him a chocolate cake. While with Portland in 1923, he had a one-run lead with two out in the ninth and the bases loaded. He raised his hand to the crowd and announced that he would strike out the Oakland hitter on a fastball, and then delivered on his promise.

Mails retired after the 1935 season to work for the San Francisco Seals. He later worked for the Giants in the public relations department. He died in 1974 at age 78.

Ray Caldwell
Pitcher, 1919–1921

Ray "Slim" Caldwell was a tall right–hander with a love for the drink. Before joining the Indians, he was fined constantly for breaking team rules and going AWOL for days at a time. Still, he was a consistent winner for his first team, the New York Highlanders, despite getting almost no run support. But the team tired of having to hire private detectives to follow their talented pitcher and, in 1919, traded Caldwell to Boston. The Red Sox wound up releasing him rather than put up with his off–field behavior.

Out of a job, Caldwell contacted Cleveland manager Tris Speaker and promised to mend his ways. Speaker told Caldwell he was welcome to join the Indians, but only if he signed a contract with a very special clause. Speaker urged the veteran pitcher to read the contract carefully. It stipulated that Caldwell was to get drunk after each game he pitched, then stay away from the park for a day. On the third day, it required that he run windsprints around League Park and, on the fourth, pitch batting practice. On the fifth, the cycle would begin again.

Caldwell rewarded Speaker's faith by going 5–1 the rest of the season. In his first start, Caldwell was one out away from a victory at League Park when a bolt of lightning struck the ground near the pitcher's mound. Caldwell was knocked unconscious for five minutes. When he came to, he assured Speaker that he could finish the game. He threw two final strikes and retired the last hitter for a 2–1 victory.

On September 10, he got revenge against one of his former teams when he threw a no–hitter against the Yankees in New York. The following year, Caldwell posted a 20–10 record and helped the Indians win the 1920 pennant. He later spent 10 seasons pitching in the minors.

Joe Sewell
Shortstop, 1920–1930

The Indians were desperate to find a new shortstop after the death of Ray Chapman. By Labor Day, with the team in a three–way fight for the pennant, Cleveland decided to take a chance on a 21–year–old player in New Orleans. They liked Joe Sewell, even though he'd spent just five months in the minors.

Although small in stature, Sewell delivered big dividends. He appeared in 22 games, hit .329 and played solid defense. He proved so reliable that he played in 1,103 consecutive games and batted .320 during 11 seasons in Cleveland.

Sewell possessed a terrific batting eye. In 7,132 games over 14 seasons, Sewell struck out just 113 times. He once played in 115 consecutive games without a single whiff and had five years where he struck out four or fewer times.

Released after the 1930 season, Sewell spent three more years in the majors with the Yankees. After retiring to his native Alabama, Sewell operated a hardware store for 20 years. In 1964, at the age of 66, he returned to his alma mater and spent seven seasons as the baseball coach at the University of Alabama. In 1977, the Veterans Committee elected Sewell to the Hall of Fame. He died in 1990 at age 91.

Charlie Jamieson
Outfielder, 1919–1932

A converted pitcher, outfielder
Charlie Jamieson came to the
Indians as the "throw–in" part of a
trade with the Athletics. By 1920,
he displaced Jack Graney as the
Indians' everyday left fielder.
Exceptionally quick with a
powerful arm, Jamieson was a fan
favorite at League Park for his
acrobatic catches.

When Tris Speaker inserted him
in the leadoff spot, Jamieson
became a hitting star, batting .316
over 14 seasons in Cleveland. In
1923, he led the American League
with 222 hits. In 1924, his .359
average was second only to Babe
Ruth's .378.

Looking back on his career,
Jamieson fondly remembered life
in the majors. "We always had two
cars of the train when we went on
the road. Half the fellows would
play cards, pinochle and checkers
all night. We used to travel on the
Pullmans at night and have our
breakfast in the hotel. We got $4 a
day for meals. We always stayed in
good hotels. Joe Wood was one of
the best pool shooters in baseball. I
used to shoot with him. Four, five
hours at a time, day in and day
out. We'd think nothing of it."

Jamieson was released by the
Indians after the 1932 season. He
returned to his native New Jersey
and worked as a security guard.

George Uhle
Pitcher, 1919–1928; 1936

In 1919, the Indians discovered George Uhle pitching semi–pro ball for his employer, the Cleveland Standard Parts Co. Uhle's team was drawing huge crowds and he commanded a percentage of the gate receipts for every game he pitched. He was making so much money that before signing with the Indians, Uhle insisted on a clause in his contract stipulating that he not be sent to the minors.

Anxious to see their $1,500 investment pay off, the Indians started Uhle against the St. Louis Browns. He won, 4–2. When he defeated St. Louis again, Uhle was in the majors to stay. He became the workhorse of the pitching staff and earned the nickname, "The Bull." He was a three–time, 20–game winner for Cleveland. His best season came in 1926, when he went 27–11 and led the league in wins, complete games and innings pitched.

Uhle was an unusually good hitter for a pitcher. He had a lifetime .288 average with nine career home runs. Traded to Detroit after the 1928 season, he locked up with White Sox ace Ted Lyons, pitching 20 innings to win a 21–inning game in 1929. His arm never recovered. Uhle returned to Cleveland in 1936 for seven games after notching his 200th, and final, career victory with the Yankees. He later coached and scouted for several years before taking a job with an ironworks company in the Cleveland area. He died in 1985.

1920 Pitching Staff
League Park

On the verge of capturing the American League pennant, the pitching staff posed for photographers at League Park. The staff was anchored by three 20–game winners. Jim Bagby, who won 31, Stanley Coveleski, who won 24, and Ray Caldwell, who won 20. Shown above are: (front row) Walter "Duster" Mails, George Cykowski, Ted Odenwald and Jim Hamilton. (Back row) Coveleski, Caldwell, Bob Clark, George Uhle, Guy Morton and Bagby. In the World Series, this group held Brooklyn's hitters to a .205 average, allowing just eight runs over seven games.

George Burns
First baseman 1920–21; 1924–28

George Burns knocked in the only run in Game 6 of the 1920 World Series. Despite hitting .361, Burns was traded the next year to the Boston Red Sox. But he returned two years later in a trade for catcher Steve O'Neill and second baseman Bill Wambsganss. Given a chance to play everyday, Burns had a career year in 1926. He led the league in hits and doubles, batted .358 and was named the league's MVP. His 64 doubles in 1926 remains the Indians' all-time single–season record.

Burns later spent five years playing and managing in the Pacific Coast League. Upon retiring from baseball, he returned to his native Seattle and spent 20 years as a deputy sheriff in King County.

Stan Coveleski
Pitcher, 1916–1924

Stanley Coveleski was the pitching hero of the 1920 World Series. He was Manager Tris Speaker's ace and was chosen to start Games 1, 4 and 7. Coveleski threw three complete games, all of them gems. He out–dueled future Hall of Famers Rube Marquard and Burleigh Grimes, and allowed the Brooklyn batters just 15 hits in 27 innings. His ERA for the series was a microscopic 0.67.

When the final out was recorded, Cleveland fans swarmed the field to congratulate their idols. Days later, over 50,000 people turned out for a ceremony in Wade Park to honor the team. The following season, the Indians trumpeted their success with the words "WORLDS CHAMPIONS" on the front of their jerseys.

Tom Manning
League Park announcer
1921–1927

Before the advent of the public address system, it was the custom at ballparks to announce the starting line-ups with a megaphone. Tom Manning, a newspaper delivery boy for *The Cleveland Press*, won a "yelling contest" and was offered the chance to put his skills to work at League Park.

In 1928, Manning traded megaphone for microphone and became the first radio announcer of Indians home games on WTAM. Manning later spent 10 years as the NBC radio network's World Series announcer. In 1938, he was chosen outstanding radio announcer by *The Sporting News*. His announcing career spanned the introduction of television and, in 1956, he spent one final year with Jimmy Dudley calling Indians games on the radio.

Sherrod Smith
Pitcher 1922–1927

"Sherry" Smith pitched for Brooklyn against the Indians in the 1920 World Series. He won Game 3, but lost Game 6 by one run to "Duster" Mails. Released on waivers two years later, Smith was picked up by Cleveland. A control pitcher who seldom walked a batter, Smith was believed to have the best "pick–off" move in baseball. Although a workhorse for Cleveland, Smith never won more than 12 games in any of six seasons with the Indians. Released in 1928, he pitched and managed in the minor leagues until 1932. He returned to Georgia and became a deputy sheriff in Newton County. Later, he worked as a prison guard until his death in 1949 at age 58.

Luke Sewell
Catcher 1921–1932; 1939

The younger brother of shortstop Joe Sewell, Luke Sewell served as a back–up catcher for five years before becoming a starter in 1926. A mediocre hitter, Sewell was traded to Washington after the 1932 season. There he caught five games in the 1933 World Series. He briefly returned to Cleveland as a player/coach in 1939 before ending his 20–year playing career. His fame came as manager of the St. Louis Browns, helping them win their only pennant in 1944. Sewell later managed the Cincinnati Reds from 1949 to 1952. He retired to Akron, Ohio, where he co–owned a bronze castings company. Sewell died in 1987 at age 86.

Johnny Hodapp
infielder 1925–1932

Debuting with the Indians at age 19, Johnny Hodapp's first years were marred by injuries. But starting in 1927, he hit over .300 four straight seasons. Hodapp put up his best numbers in 1930, when he led the league in hits and doubles, and hit .354. Never a good fielder, he was traded to the White Sox in 1932. After nine years in the major leagues, Hodapp returned to his native Cincinnati to help with the family mortuary business. He died of cancer in 1980.

Glenn Myatt
Catcher 1923–1935

Glenn Myatt spent 13 years with the Indians, but was the everyday catcher for only two. After batting .342 in 1924, Myatt's average dropped and he lost the job to Luke Sewell in 1926. Released early in 1935 at age 37, Myatt sent telegrams to other clubs, looking for one last chance. Only Bill Terry of the Giants expressed interest. In his first at bat with New York, Myatt delivered a bases-loaded triple. "It was the most gratifying hit of my life," he later recalled. Myatt later returned to his native Houston, where he died in 1969.

Joe Shaute
Pitcher 1922–1930

Joe Shaute (pronounced Shay-oot) came from the coal–mining country of eastern Pennsylvania. He had planned to become a teacher, but when he was spotted pitching by former Cleveland star Charles Hickman, then mayor of Morgantown, W. Va., he was signed to a contract on the spot. The first batter he faced with Cleveland was Babe Ruth, whom he struck out on four pitches. Shaute struck Ruth out more than 30 times during his career. Ruth would exact revenge during the 1927 season, when he hit three of 60 homers off Shaute.

Shaute's best season was 1924, when he won 20 games for the sixth–place Indians. After three final seasons with Brooklyn, Shaute returned to the Scranton area where he spent three years pitching and managing in the minors. Later elected sheriff of Lackawanna County, he became part–owner of a hosiery mill.

Mrs. Jim Dunn and Tris Speaker
League Park, 1926

When Indians owner Jim Dunn died in 1922, ownership of the team passed to his widow, Edith. Mrs. Dunn was the first woman to own an American League franchise. She kept Tris Speaker as manager and delegated club operations to E.S. Barnard, who later became president of the American League.

At the time this photo was taken, Mrs. Dunn and Speaker had little time left with the team. Late in 1926, allegations surfaced that Speaker and Tiger great Ty Cobb had placed a bet on the Cleveland–Detroit game the final day of the 1919 season. The plan was for the Indians to allow the Tigers to win the game and finish in third place ahead of the Yankees. The Tiger players would then pick up the additional bonus money paid out by the league. The plan failed as Cleveland won the game.

Commissioner Landis cleared both players, despite written evidence implicating them. Weeks later, Speaker resigned as manager and signed with Washington for the 1927 season. Cobb also suddenly changed teams, going to Philadelphia.

Mrs. Dunn would sell the Indians to developer Alva Bradley the following November.

Alva Bradley
Owner 1927–1946

The son of a wealthy Cleveland industrialist, Alva Bradley headed a group of prominent businessmen who purchased the Indians for $1 million from Mrs. Dunn. Bradley and his group spent money to improve League Park. They hired former umpire Billy Evans to oversee baseball operations and launched the effort to build Municipal Stadium on the lakefront. The new owners viewed the purchase of the club as an act of civic responsibility, since they all had other sources of income. A great fan of the game, Bradley was a fixture at League Park, often visiting the team in the locker room after home games.

But for all their deep pockets, the 20–year tenure of Bradley's ownership group never produced a team that finished better than third place. In 1946, Bradley's partners negotiated the sale of the team to Bill Veeck. Bradley never recovered from the shock of losing the team. He died in 1953 in Florida at age 69.

Lew Fonseca
First baseman 1927–1931

Lew Fonseca was a first-rate hitter, but both the Reds and the Phillies gave up on him because he was constantly injured. In 1927, Cleveland took a chance on him and it paid off. Fonseca won the American League batting title in 1929, hitting .369. But that winter, he nearly died from scarlet fever and was traded to the White Sox early in the 1931 season. There, he served as player/manager from 1932 to 1934.

In retirement, Lew Fonseca made his most lasting contribution to the game. He created the first highlight film from home movies shot to help his teammates analyze their hitting. Fonseca produced the first sound films of the 1935 World Series and All-Star Game, and then distributed them to schools and church groups to help publicize the game. During World War II, millions of GIs were shown Fonseca's movies as morale boosters. By the late 1950s, it was estimated that the films had been seen by more than 250 million people. He died in 1989 at age 90.

Roger Peckinpaugh
Manager, 1928–1933; 1941

As a child in Cleveland, Roger Peckinpaugh lived on Hough Avenue, across the street from his boyhood idol, Napoleon Lajoie. As a player, Peckinpaugh spent 17 years as a shortstop, mostly with the Yankees and the Senators. He appeared in three World Series and was named the 1925 American League MVP. When his playing career ended with the White Sox in 1927, Cleveland wanted him to come home as manager. Chicago refused to let him go until paid $12,500.

Despite the financial resources of Cleveland's new owners and the arrival of several quality players, the new manager could deliver no better than third place in 1929, a distant 24 games behind the powerhouse Philadelphia Athletics. When the team finished fourth the next three seasons and got off to a terrible start in 1933, Cleveland fans clamored for a change. Peckinpaugh was fired on June 9 and replaced by Walter Johnson, who had turned to managing after an All–Star pitching career.

Peckinpaugh would return to the Indians in 1941 as manager for one year, then move into the front office as general manager through 1946. He died in Cleveland in 1977 at age 86.

Wes Ferrell
Pitcher, 1927–1933

Wesley Cheek Ferrell possessed a blazing fastball and an even hotter temper. Signed out of his native North Carolina at age 19, Ferrell won 20 games for Terre Haute in 1928 and quickly established himself as the ace of the Indians staff by 1929. He was a 20–game winner for four straight seasons, but it was his explosive demeanor on the mound that grabbed the headlines. Ferrell would show displeasure by destroying his glove, kicking water coolers, stomping on his wristwatch and, once, refusing to leave the mound. Ferrell would regularly destroy a deck of cards when he didn't like the hand he was dealt. He was an annual hold–out at contract time and was repeatedly fined for his outbursts. But his teammates loved his fiery attitude. Red Sox teammate Bill Werber recalled, "He hated to lose, at anything."

Blessed with matinee–idol looks, Ferrell was also a superb hitter. A career .280 hitter, he had 38 career home runs, including nine in 1931 for the Indians. On April 29, 1931, he threw a no–hitter against the Browns at League Park, adding a home run and knocking in four runs for good measure. When the Indians thought his best years were behind him, they traded Ferrell to Boston in 1934. It was a terrible miscalculation. Adding off–speed pitches to his repertoire, Ferrell rebounded to win 25 games in 1935 and lead the league in wins, innings pitched and complete games. In 1936, he won another 20 games. But at 28, his arm was shot. He won 15 games in 1938, his last full season.

Returning to his Carolina home, Ferrell managed several teams during the war years and his fiery ways continued. He was suspended a full year for slugging an umpire and, later, fined for yanking his team off the field in the middle of a game. Ferrell died in 1976 at age 68.

Grover Hartley
Catcher, 1929–1930

Grover Hartley was 40 when he arrived in Cleveland. A veteran of 12 big-league seasons, all as a backup catcher, Hartley was renowned for his handling of young pitchers. Originally hired as a coach for the 1928 season, Hartley was pressed into playing 25 games during his two years with the Indians. He became a coach with the Pirates for three years and, later, the Browns, from 1934 to 1936.

Eddie Morgan
First baseman, 1928–1933

Eddie Morgan's bat kept him in the Indians lineup. Originally an outfielder, Morgan proved a defensive liability and was moved to first base. He responded by hitting over .300 his first four seasons and had his best year in 1930, batting .349 with 26 home runs. But when his average dropped, he was traded to the Red Sox in 1934 to make room for a young Hal Trosky at first base. Morgan retired after one final season and returned to New Orleans to work in his family's box business.

Mel "Chief" Harder
Pitcher, 1928–1947

When he arrived at the Indians training camp in 1928, Melvin LeRoy Harder was a skinny 18–year old with a tale to tell. He had won 13 games in eight weeks for Dubuque, pitching every third day. Manager Roger Peckinpaugh was impressed, but knew that such a schedule was far too stressful for the arm of a youngster who weighed only 140 pounds. The Indians decided to keep young Harder, get his weight up and give him a chance to observe big–league hitters. Under orders to drink two quarts of milk a day and eat all the spinach he could stomach, Harder sat on the bench. Sent back to the minors in 1929, Harder perfected a curveball that got him back in the Indians rotation for 1930.

On July 31, 1932, Harder pitched the first game at the new Municipal Stadium, but lost to the Athletics and Lefty Grove, 1–0. In 1934, he won 20 games and pitched in the All–Star game. His 22–11 record in 1935 would be his best and lead to another All–Star appearance. Midway through 1936, on his way to another superb year, Harder developed bursitis in his shoulder and was forced to end the season with just 15 wins. Despite being plagued by arm pain for the rest of his career, Harder managed to win 223 games for the Indians. After the 1947 season, he became the Indians' pitching coach, a position he held until 1963. In 1990, the Indians retired Harder's number "18."

Willis Hudlin
Pitcher, 1926–1940

The Yankees had a chance to sign Willis Hudlin out of high school, before he joined the Indians for a long pitching career. The Yankees would regret the oversight because Hudlin came to be known as a "Yankee Killer," defeating Babe Ruth and his teammates 14 times over three seasons. Ruth would get a small measure of revenge in 1929 when he hit his 500th career home run off Hudlin at League Park.

A side–arm sinkerball pitcher, Hudlin won 157 games for Cleveland. Released early in the 1940 season, Hudlin pitched briefly for three teams before becoming player/manager for Little Rock from 1941 to 1946. Later, he became pitching coach for the Tigers before becoming a scout for the Yankees.

Dick Porter
Outfielder, 1929–1934

Dick Porter possessed an unorthodox batting style that made baseball scouts doubtful of his major league potential. Standing at the plate, Porter would wiggle his body and wave his bat like a wand. It earned him the nickname "Twitchy." Despite hitting over .300 for six straight years in the minors, teams were convinced his approach would never prove successful against major-league pitching. In 1929, Indians General Manager Billy Evans, desperate to improve on his team's seventh-place finish, took a chance and paid $40,000 to buy Porter from Baltimore of the International League.

Evans was rewarded with a left-handed hitter who hit over .300 his first four years in Cleveland. In 1934, Porter was traded to Boston, but soon found himself back in the minors, where he went on to manage. He died in 1974 at age 73.

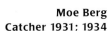

Moe Berg
Catcher 1931; 1934

Moe Berg is best remembered for his off-field behavior. A career back-up catcher who played just 39 games for Cleveland over parts of two seasons, Berg was a scholarly player. A graduate of Princeton, he spoke 12 languages, studied in Paris and earned a law degree from Columbia University. He purchased foreign-language newspapers and closely guarded them, believing they were "alive." He warned teammates not to disturb them until they had been read and rendered "dead." A true eccentric, he bathed two or three times daily. He never married, never learned to drive a car, and never wore anything but a black suit

Berg was involved in espionage for the U.S. government during World War II. Traveling to Japan in 1934 with Babe Ruth and other players, he secretly photographed Tokyo. His rooftop photos were later used by the U. S. Air Force to plan bombing missions. Later, posing as a German citizen, he traveled through Europe gathering information on the progress of Germany's atomic research. Berg was a frequent guest at embassy parties in Washington and was close friends with Albert Einstein and Will Rogers. He was a regular contestant on nationally syndicated radio quiz shows.

Earl Averill
Outfielder, 1929–1939

Earl Averill's career was a lesson in perseverance. He was laughed out of the San Francisco Seals tryout camp at age 22 because he was considered too small. But Averill played semi–pro ball long enough and well enough to join the Seals four years later. There, for three straight seasons, he averaged over .320 and hit more than 20 home runs. When Indians General Manager Billy Evans needed outfield help, he scouted two of Averill's teammates, but on the recommendation of several former Bay area big leaguers, purchased Averill instead for $45,000.

Averill hit a home run in his first at bat and was an instant hit with the Indians. To reduce his effectiveness as a left–handed pull–hitter, other teams employed an early version of the "Ted Williams shift" against him, sending the shortstop to the right side of second base. It had little effect on the stubborn Averill, who later remarked, "I played five or six seasons before I found out there were three fields to hit the ball to." Taking advantage of the short right–field wall at League Park, Averill hit 226 home runs for Cleveland, the team record until Albert Belle hit 242.

A six–time All–Star, Averill felt a sudden numbness in his legs midway through the 1937 season. X–rays revealed a spinal defect that forced him to alter his batting style. The result was a sharp drop in his power numbers. Traded to Detroit in June 1939, Averill soon became a part–time player and later retired to his hometown of Snohomish, Washington, where he operated a hotel for many years. The Veterans Committee elected Averill to the Hall of Fame in 1975. His number "3" was retired by the Indians that same year.

Joe Vosmik
Outfielder, 1930–1936

As a youngster, Joe Vosmik repeatedly skipped school to sneak into games at League Park. He was such a regular that the stadium guards and truant officers knew him by name. Discovered playing sandlot ball, Vosmik returned to the ballpark permanently in 1931 when he debuted as a rookie with the Indians. After going five-for-five in the second game of the season, he became the everyday left fielder and finished the year with a .320 average.

For the next five years, Vosmik and Earl Averill gave the Indians one of the league's most lethal hitting tandems. Vosmik's best year was 1935, when he led the league in hits, doubles and triples, and batted .348. That year, the All-Star crowd at Municipal Stadium gave their hometown hero a two-minute ovation when he was introduced.

After a sub-par year in 1936, when his average dipped to .287, Vosmik was traded to the St. Louis Browns. Cleveland fans were livid about the trade and threatened to boycott games in protest. In St. Louis, Vosmik quickly found his old form and hit .325 and .324 for two seasons, leading the league with 201 hits in 1938. By 1940, at age 30, leg injuries slowed Vosmik and he was no longer an everyday player. He spent four years playing in the American Association before becoming a manager in the Indians minor league system. He later returned to Cleveland and worked as a department store salesman. Vosmik died after an operation for lung cancer in 1962 at age 51.

Bill Cissell and Willie Kamm
League Park, 1932

Chicago White Sox owner Charles Comiskey paid $100,000 for third baseman Willie Kamm in 1922 and, in 1927, the same amount for infielder Bill Cissell. Both players were solid performers, but neither ever justified their record price tags. In 1931, the White Sox dealt Kamm to Cleveland, where he spent the next four years as the everyday third baseman. A terrific glove man, Kamm was famous for pulling his "hidden ball" trick on unsuspecting baserunners. But he feuded with Manager Walter Johnson and was released in 1935. After briefly managing in the minors, Kamm, who had invested wisely in the stock market, retired a wealthy man.

Cissell spent four years as the White Sox shortstop before he was traded to Cleveland in 1932 and moved to second base. Freed from huge expectations, he had a career year and batted .320. But an appendicitis attack slowed him in 1934 and he was traded to the Red Sox. He played and managed in the minors until 1941, then drifted around the country before landing back in Chicago, where he was discovered destitute and gravely ill by a reporter in 1949. When White Sox Vice President Charles Comiskey, grandson of the man who had purchased Cissell in 1928, heard of Cissell's plight, he paid all of his medical expenses and two months later, his funeral expenses.

Monte Pearson
Pitcher, 1932–1935

The Indians purchased Monte Pearson for $20,000 after he won 17 games for his hometown Oakland Oaks in the Pacific Coast League in 1931. Proclaimed a "can't miss" prospect by the Cleveland brass, Pearson won 10 games for the Indians in 1933, led the league with a 2.33 ERA and appeared on his way to stardom. But once he complained of a sore arm, he fell out of favor with Manager Walter Johnson. When he won just eight games in 1935, he was traded to the Yankees for pitcher Johnny Allen.

Once in New York and teamed with the Yankees' vaunted offense, Pearson notched a career-high 19 victories in 1936. The following season, he threw a no-hitter against the Indians. From 1936 to 1939, Pearson pitched one game in four straight World Series and won all four games. But his constant arm ailments got him branded a hypochondriac by the New York press. He retired after the 1941 season and moved to Fresno, California, where he worked for the county sanitation department.

Thornton Lee
Pitcher, 1933–1936

Thornton Lee was a tall, lanky left-hander whose career blossomed after he left Cleveland. Unable to crack the Indians starting rotation, Lee was used mostly as a reliever before being traded to the White Sox in 1937. There, the Chicago coaches corrected a flaw in his delivery and made him a starter. For the next five years, Lee was one of the most effective pitchers in the American League. In 1941, he won 22 games, threw 30 complete games and led the league with a 2.37 ERA. Recurring arm problems haunted him, however, and he retired to Arizona after the 1948 season. He died in 1997 at age 90.

Walter Johnson
Manager, 1933–1935

When the Indians were looking to replace Roger Peckinpaugh as manager, they thought they had found the ideal candidate in Walter Johnson, a Hall of Fame pitcher who managed the Washington Senators for four years, winning more than 90 games three times.

Cleveland sportswriters drummed up fan support and expectations were high for a team that had finished fourth three straight times. But when the team finished fourth again in 1933, criticism of the new manager started to grow. Johnson couldn't understand why his pitchers couldn't duplicate what had come so easily for him. Several players chafed under Johnson and, after he sent two popular players home for insubordination, the fans and press turned against him. A third-place finish in 1934 didn't satisfy anyone and soon, Johnson and the newspaper writers stopped talking to each other. With the fans staying away in record numbers, owner Alva Bradley bowed to the pressure and replaced Johnson with Steve O'Neill in August 1935.

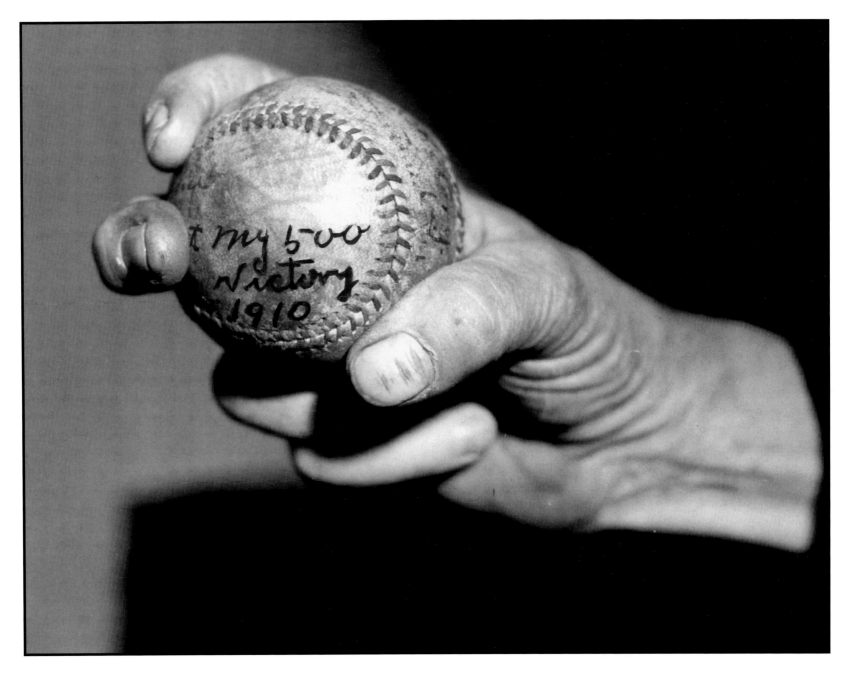

Cy Young's 500th Win Ball
1935

In 1935, a photographer traveled to the Ohio farm of 68–year–old pitching great Cy Young, who had retired more than 20 years earlier. Young proudly showed his guest a souvenir of his career, the baseball he saved from an historic win in Cleveland.

Inscribed on the ball, in black ink, were the words: "My 500 victory, 1910." Young's lifetime record of 511 victories is unsurpassed, a record that should endure for the ages.

Hal Trosky
First baseman, 1933–1941

Hal Trosky played in an era of great first basemen in the American League. Though overshadowed by Lou Gehrig and Hank Greenberg, Trosky had a sensational rookie season in 1934. He hit .330 with 35 home runs and 142 RBIs. He drove in more than 100 runs for six straight years.

In 1936, Trosky had a monumental year. His 162 RBIs set the Indians' single-season record until broken by Manny Ramirez's 165 in 1999. In his first seven full seasons, Trosky hit 204 home runs and drove in 852 runs.

But at age 28 and at the height of his career, Trosky was forced into early retirement because of severe migraine headaches. He returned to his Iowa farm. In 1944, he briefly returned to the majors with the Chicago White Sox for parts of two seasons, but his skills had eroded. Trosky became a scout for the White Sox. He died in 1979 at age 66.

Cy Slapnicka and Bruce Campbell
League Park, 1936

Cyril "Cy" Slapnicka, Cleveland's chief scout for more than 20 years, is best remembered for getting the signature of 17–year old Bob Feller on a Cleveland contract. Slapnicka signed most of the Indians' star players over the years, including pitcher Mel Harder, first baseman Hal Trosky, third baseman Ken Keltner and pitcher Herb Score. Slapnicka was the team's general manager from 1936 to 1941.

Bruce Campbell joined Cleveland in 1935 as a right fielder. He was hitting .325 in early August when he developed spinal meningitis and almost died. Despite being stricken twice again in 1936 and 1938, Campbell miraculously recovered to play three full seasons, before being traded to Detroit in 1940.

William and Bob Feller
1936

As a youngster growing up near Van Meter, Iowa, Bob Feller demonstrated talent with a baseball at an early age. His father, William, built a make–shift ballfield on the family farm and organized a local boys' team, the Oak Views. Young Bob was the Oak Views' star attraction. At 16, he traveled to the national amateur tournament in Dayton, Ohio, where he attracted the attention of major league scouts. Indians scout Cy Slapnicka, a fellow Iowan, convinced Feller's father to let his son sign a contract for $500 to pitch for Fargo–Moorhead, a minor league team in the Indians farm system. But Feller never made it to the minors. A much bigger assignment came first

Bob Feller
League Park, 1936

When the high school year ended, 17–year–old Bob Feller was called to Cleveland. There, he pitched one game for a local semi–pro team, the Rosenblums. The day after his minor league debut, Feller was tapped to pitch in an exhibition game against the visiting St. Louis Cardinals.

On July 6, during the All–Star break, the infamous "Gas House Gang" came to League Park. Indians pitcher George Uhle threw the first three innings. Bob Feller faced nine batters over the next three innings. To everyone's amazement, he struck out eight of them. Afterwards, Cardinals ace Dizzy Dean was asked if he'd pose for a picture with the young Feller. Dean responded, "Why ask me? Ask that kid if he'll pose with me." Feller threw one more semi–pro game before joining the Indians full–time.

Bob Feller
Pitcher, 1936–1941; 1945–1956

At the height of the Depression, the nation was hungry for heroes and the sudden arrival of Bob Feller provided instant headlines for the nation's newspapers. Feller struck out 15 Browns in his first major–league start. Three weeks later, he matched Dizzy Dean's major–league record of 17 strikeouts. The press dubbed him "Rapid Robert" because of his blazing speed.

Feller was an instant celebrity. Attendance soared as fans flocked to ballparks to catch a look at the young phenom. He was flooded with endorsement offers. He finished the 1936 season with five wins in eight starts and struck out 76 batters in 62 innings. That fall, Feller returned to Iowa and began his senior year of high school. He was still just 17.

Odell "Bad News" Hale
Infielder, 1931; 1933–1940

In the minors, Arvel Odell Hale once hit seven home runs in six days, leading opposing players to nickname him "Bad News." With the Indians, he twice drove in more than 100 runs and for four years, batted .300 or better. In 1935, while playing third base, he participated in an unusual triple play. A line drive glanced off his glove and hit him in the head, but was caught in the air by shortstop Bill Knickerbocker for one out. Knickerbocker threw to the second baseman who relayed it to first, doubling off both baserunners. "I'm the only player who ever used his head in a triple play," Hale recalled. He later retired to Arkansas and worked in the oil refining business.

Lyn Lary
Shortstop, 1937–1939

Lynford Hobart Lary was a member of the 1930's Yankee dynasty for five years and was nicknamed "Broadway" by teammate Babe Ruth for his love of the theater. The Yankees traded Lary and he played for six teams in the next seven years. He was the Indians' regular shortstop for two seasons before moving to Brooklyn early in 1939. He fell in love with a Broadway actress who he married, divorced and re–married, the second time for 42 years, until his death in 1973.

Johnny Allen
Pitcher, 1936–1940

Johnny Allen was a pitcher with overpowering stuff and a temper to match. Allen earned a reputation with the Yankees for challenging everything and everyone. Raised in a North Carolina orphanage, Allen was nicknamed "The Tarheel Typhoon" for his outbursts. He constantly fought with manager Joe McCarthy, questioned umpires' calls, berated teammates and was a regular holdout at contract time. Teammate Lou Gehrig recalled, "The guy thinks he should win every time he pitches and if he loses, it's a personal conspiracy against him." Despite a record of 50-19 over his first four seasons, the Yankees tired of his antics and traded him to the Indians after the 1935 season.

In Cleveland, the winning and the tantrums continued. In 1936, Allen won 20 games for the Indians, but there was a price to pay. After a loss in Boston, Allen trashed a hotel bar and assaulted a hotel employee with a fire extinguisher. At the ballpark, he was repeatedly ejected for threatening umpires and he became the object of severe "bench-jockeying" by rival dugouts. Opposing teams learned they could distract Allen by asking the umpire to keep checking his pitches for spitballs. Despite the turmoil, Allen was even more dominating in 1937. He went 15-0 despite missing two months recuperating from an appendectomy. The only blemish on his record occurred on the final day of the season. He lost 1-0 to Detroit's Jake Wade, who held the Indians to one hit.

In 1938, Allen had 12 wins when he suffered an arm injury in the All-Star game. He would never win more than 10 games in any of his remaining six years. But the old fire never left him. In 1943, while pitching for Brooklyn, Allen was fined and suspended for attacking umpire George Barr, who called him for a balk. Ironically, Allen later spent four seasons as a minor league umpire in the Carolinas.

Al Milnar
Pitcher, 1936; 1938–1943

A product of Cleveland–area sandlots, Al Milnar struck out 24 batters in a single game at age 16. His father, a Slovenian immigrant who operated a neighborhood candy store, sponsored his son's semi–pro team, the Sweets. When young Milnar struck out 18 Indians in an exhibition game in Zanesville, the big left–hander was sent to Cleveland's top farm team in New Orleans, where he won 46 games in two seasons. But wildness kept him from becoming a regular with the Indians until 1939. He had a career year in 1940, when he won 18 games with four shutouts and pitched a string of 24 scoreless innings.

Ken Keltner
Third baseman, 1937–1949

The Indians took Ken Keltner to spring training in 1938, after bringing him up from Milwaukee for a late-season look at the end of 1937. In his two minor league seasons, Ken Keltner hit 60 home runs, batted .333 and knocked in 213 RBIs. Cleveland sent Milwaukee $35,000 and three players to buy his contract. The payoff was immediate. In his first year, Keltner produced 26 home runs and 113 RBIs, leading the team in both. In 1939, he hit .325 with 37 doubles.

Keltner's defensive play was equally impressive. A seven-time All-Star, he annually ranked among the league's elite fielders. His power numbers declined during the war years, but in 1948, his 31 home runs and 119 RBIs helped propel the Indians to the pennant. His three-run homer in the one-game playoff at Boston put the Tribe in the World Series.

In 1949, Keltner was released to make room for a young Al Rosen at third base. He retired to his native Milwaukee and worked as a sales rep for an industrial supply company. He died in 1991 at age 75.

Roy "Stormy" Weatherly
Outfielder, 1936–1942

Cyril Roy Weatherly was nicknamed "Stormy" because he constantly argued with umpires and was often thrown out of games. The trait seemed to run in the family. During a game at League Park in 1936, Weatherly was called out on a close play at first base. His father, sitting in the first base stands on "Dad's Day," jumped over the railing with a bead on the umpire. He had to be restrained. The senior Weatherly was startled to learn anyone found his actions strange, commenting, "If my boy's in trouble, I'm going to help him. I don't care where it is."

In 1940, Indians owner Alva Bradley offered "Stormy" a $500 bonus if he could make it through the season without a single ejection. Weatherly collected. It was Weatherly's fielding that kept him in the majors for parts of ten seasons. The diminutive Texan was a speedy flycatcher as the Indians' fourth outfielder. He was traded to the Yankees after the 1942 season. Weatherly later served as a paratrooper in Europe during World War II.

Jeff Heath
Outfielder, 1936–1945

Jeff Heath was a standout high school football player who turned down several college scholarships to pursue a career in baseball. Blessed with the upper body of a blacksmith, Heath was supremely confident in his abilities. After tearing up the minor leagues for two seasons, Heath held out in 1938 when he couldn't come to terms with Cleveland management. Each day during spring training, Heath would sit in the stands and watch the Indians practice. When veteran Hal Trosky, who'd hit 74 home runs over the previous two seasons, chided him, "Why don't you quit stalling? Sign your contract and get to work like the rest of us!" Heath had a ready answer. "Listen, if you could hit like me, Trosky, you'd hold out all season." All this from a rookie who'd appeared in 32 big–league games.

Once he finally signed his contract, Heath backed up his words with 21 home runs, 112 RBIs and a .343 average. And he led the league in triples. But when he failed to repeat his rookie performance the next season, he gained a reputation as a loafer.

Heath was temperamental and highly superstitious. He didn't want anyone using his bats. "There are only so many hits in a bat," he declared, "and I want them to be mine." Manager Oscar Vitt believed Heath could be a superstar if he tried harder. They feuded constantly. Heath helped lead the players' revolt against Vitt during the 1940 season, a stunt that earned the team the tag "Cleveland Crybabies." After Vitt was fired at season's end, Heath had the best year of his career in 1941.

Traded after the 1945 season, Heath finished his career with the Browns and the Braves. He retired to the Seattle area, spent several seasons broadcasting Seattle Rainiers games and later went into real estate. He died of a heart attack at age 59 in 1975.

Oscar Vitt
Manager, 1938–1940

Oscar Vitt spent 10 seasons as an infielder and teammate of Ty Cobb in Detroit and Babe Ruth in Boston. But it was as a manager in the minors and later in Cleveland that Vitt achieved notoriety. After 11 years in the Pacific Coast League, Vitt was given control of the Yankees' top farm club, the Newark Bears, which was loaded with future major leaguers. Many consider the 1937 Newark club, which won 109 games, the greatest minor league team of all time.

Cleveland's owners thought Vitt's aggressive style was the solution for a team that had finished no higher than third place since 1926. So they hired him. But the Indians finished third again under Vitt in 1938 and 1939, and fans and players alike grew frustrated. Vitt openly blamed his players. In the newspapers, he questioned their ability. From the bench, he made insulting comments.

When the Indians reached first place in June 1940, the players decided to openly challenge Vitt. About a dozen players met with team owner Alva Bradley on June 13 and asked that Vitt be fired. Bradley asked for time to consider the request, but promised nothing. When news of the meeting was leaked to the newspapers, the players were seen as "soft." A columnist coined a term that stuck: "Crybabies." Bradley decided to stick by his manager and, as the team traveled around the league, the players faced ridicule. Rival fans began hanging baby bottles over the railings and opposing teams taunted the Indians players with insults. For their part, the Indians held onto first place through late August, but suddenly slumped and finished second to Detroit by a single game. Cleveland fans would have to wait eight years for another pennant race.

Vitt was replaced by Roger Peckinpaugh as manager the following season. He never managed again.

Ken Keltner
Terminal Tower, 1938

In the summer of 1938, third baseman Ken Keltner ascended to the top of Cleveland's tallest landmark to help set a world record. With five teammates stationed below, Keltner began dropping baseballs, 12 in all. Two found their way into the mitts of catchers Frankie Pytlak and Hank Helf. The drop was measured at 708 feet, although later accounts disputed the figure. However, it was agreed that the drop broke the previous record set in 1908 by Washington Senators catcher "Gabby" Street, who caught a ball dropped 504 feet from the observation deck of the Washington Monument.

Oscar Vitt and Johnny Allen
Yankee Stadium, 1938

Temperamental pitcher Johnny Allen never took direction very well. On June 7, 1938, Allen was facing the Red Sox at Fenway Park with umpire Bill McGowan behind home plate. McGowan had ejected Allen from a game earlier in the season for arguing balls and strikes. Now Allen was again questioning McGowan's eyesight. When Red Sox hitter Joe Cronin complained that the sleeve of Allen's undershirt was frayed and distracted him as he hit, umpire McGowan ordered Allen to change undershirts or be ejected from the game. Allen headed for the Indians clubhouse. When he failed to return, Indians manager

Vitt went to investigate.

Allen was challenging McGowan's order. He refused to pitch without the undershirt. Vitt fined Allen $250 and replaced him with another pitcher. For several days, Cleveland newspapers wrote about the incident and the undershirt became an object of much curiosity. Indians owner Alva Bradley had a solution. His brother, who owned the Higbee and Company department store, offered Allen $250 for the offending garment. A deal was struck and the store proudly displayed the shirt in its show–room window for all to see.

Joe Heving
Pitcher, 1937–38; 1941–44

Joe Heving didn't reach the majors until he was 30 years old. Branded a reliever by Giants manager John McGraw, the label stuck and Heving spent 13 seasons pitching almost exclusively out of the bullpen. A sinkerball pitcher, Heving complained constantly about the lack of regular work that came with being a reliever. His best year with Cleveland came in 1944, when he led the league with 63 appearances, had eight saves and a miserly 1.96 ERA.

Oscar Grimes
Infielder, 1938–1942

Oscar Grimes could play any infield position well, but his career as an everyday player was cut short by a freak injury. In May 1940, during an afternoon practice, Grimes was hit in the face by a line drive off the bat of teammate Odell "Bad News" Hale. The ball fractured Grimes' cheekbone and nearly blinded him. He was never a regular with the Indians again.

Released after the 1942 season, Grimes spent parts of the next four years with the Yankees. After another few years in the minors, he retired to work for Republic Steel as a millwright during the 1950s.

Rollie Hemsley
Catcher, 1938–1941

Ralston Burdett Hemsley is best remembered for nearly drinking himself out of baseball. Nicknamed "Rollicking Rollie" for his post–game antics, he seemed to be constantly engaged in bar–room brawls. "I had so many black eyes," he once said, "that my friends thought I was born with them." Hemsley played for four major league teams in 10 years before arriving in Cleveland in 1938. Drinking got him suspended twice in his first season. When he terrorized a late–night train trip at the start of the 1939 season, Indians management had seen enough.

Shipped back to Cleveland, Hemsley was met at the train platform by two businessmen who carted him off to an Akron hospital. There, he was told the story of a new group— Alcoholics Anonymous. The four–day stay changed his life.

Returning to the Indians, the veteran Hemsley helped tutor Bob Feller and caught his opening day no–hitter in 1940. Hemsley was sold to the Reds after the 1941 season and spent another six years in the majors, all as a back–up catcher. Hemsley later managed in the minors and was a scout for the Athletics and the Senators.

Ben Chapman
Outfielder, 1939–1940

Ben Chapman is best remembered for what he did before he joined the Indians and for what he did once he left. Prior to his arrival in Cleveland, Chapman, a career .302 hitter, spent six years as an everyday outfielder for the great Yankee teams of the 1930s. Four times he led the league in stolen bases and four times he was named to the All-Star team.

In 1936, New York traded Chapman to make room for Joe DiMaggio. In 1939, he came to Cleveland for two years, hitting three triples in a game his first season.

Chapman went on to manage in the minor leagues but in 1943, he was suspended for the entire season for punching an umpire. His fiery style was thought to be the antidote needed by the hapless Phillies, who named him player/manager during the 1945 season.

Chapman had a controversial tenure in Philadelphia. When Jackie Robinson debuted with the Brooklyn Dodgers in 1947, he was the object of vicious verbal attacks by opposing teams, none more so than Chapman's Phillies. The constant racial taunting was once followed by the release of a black cat on the playing field while Robinson was at bat.

As a southerner from Alabama, Chapman was unapologetic for his team's behavior. He later recalled, "I'm not ashamed of anything that happened. I wasn't then, and I'm not now. Our purpose was to win, and if we could do that by getting a rookie rattled, we would."

George Case
Outfielder, 1946

George Case was universally regarded as the fastest major league player of his era. He led the American League in stolen bases six times. But by the time Case joined the Indians in 1946, leg and back injuries had slowed him down. He played just one more season before retiring.

While with Cleveland, Case raced Olympic hero Jessie Owens in a 100-yard dash in one of owner Bill Veeck's first promotional stunts. Owens, in a track suit, edged out Case, in full uniform, by one-tenth of a second on the grass surface of Municipal Stadium.

In 1951, Case began 10 seasons as the baseball coach at Rutgers University. He later managed in the minors and was a scout for several major league teams.

Bob Lemon
League Park, 1942

Bob Lemon began his career in Cleveland in 1941 as a third baseman, known for a strong arm but weak bat. He had just nine at–bats in his first two trials with the Indians, and after two years, left for World War II and three years in the Navy.

When Lemon returned in 1946, Ken Keltner had become a fixture at third base. The Indians sent Lemon to the outfield because of his exceptionally strong arm, but he proved a weak hitter. Out of desperation, he was given a trial in the bullpen as a relief pitcher. Taught to pitch by veteran Mel Harder, Lemon became a winner and within two years, a regular in the rotation. Lemon's pitches had a natural sinking effect. Even bouts of wildness couldn't derail his development. He became one of the league's most dominant pitchers. In 1948, the former outfielder won 20 games and threw a no–hitter against Detroit. The conversion from hitter to pitcher was complete.

Lou Boudreau
Shortstop, 1938–1950
Manager, 1942–1950

Slick fielding launched Lou Boudreau to the majors, but it was his on-field leadership abilities that proved his greatest asset. Boudreau's hard-nosed play and hitting earned him the respect of teammates considerably older. In 1940, at age 22, he hit .295, drove in 101 runs and made the All-Star team. Despite two weak ankles that made him ineligible for military service, Boudreau led the league in doubles three times and, in 1944, won the batting title with a .327 average.

In 1942, the Indians named the 24-year old Boudreau as manager and the media dubbed him the "Boy manager." The loss of several key players to the war effort had left Cleveland with a second-rate team. In Boudreau's first five seasons as manager, the team finished higher than fourth only once. When Bill Veeck purchased the Indians in 1946, he had doubts about Boudreau as manager. Only a huge outcry of fan support kept Veeck from replacing him. Boudreau came back with his most inspired play, batting a career-high .355 and being named league MVP. His two home runs in the playoff game against the Red Sox gave Cleveland its first pennant in almost 30 years.

Released by the Indians after the 1950 season, Boudreau played one season for the Red Sox and then managed the team for three. He later managed the Kansas City Athletics and the Chicago Cubs, the latter after becoming a baseball broadcaster in Chicago. In 1970, Boudreau was elected to the Hall of Fame.

Allie Reynolds
Pitcher, 1942–1946

Allie Reynolds led the league in strikeouts his first full season with Cleveland. In 1945, he won 18 games and appeared positioned to become a cornerstone of the Indians' starting staff. But when Bill Veeck bought the team in 1946, things changed for Reynolds. Veeck coveted the Yankees' second baseman, Joe Gordon, and learned he was available. The price: Reynolds.

The deal helped both teams. Gordon cemented the Indians' infield and provided needed power. Reynolds gave the Yankees six straight seasons of 16 or more wins, including 1951, when he threw two no–hitters in the same season, one against the Indians. In 1952, he won 20 games and led the American League in ERA, strikeouts and shutouts. Reynolds, who was born in Oklahoma of Creek Indian descent, became one of the Yankees' most dependable postseason pitchers. The New York media nicknamed him "Superchief."

Hal Peck
Outfielder, 1947–1949

Hal Peck's major league career almost never happened. In the minors in 1942, Peck lost two toes in a hunting accident. But fitted with a special shoe, he came back and hit over .330 for Milwaukee the next two seasons.

In Milwaukee, owner Bill Veeck sold Peck to the Philadelphia Athletics for a reported $50,000. Four years later, Veeck brought Peck to Cleveland. After one season as the Indians' regular right fielder, an arm injury caused him to become a pinch hitter. In 1948, he led the league in pinch hits. He retired in 1949 to his native Wisconsin and worked as a sales representative for an oil company. He died in 1995.

Steve Gromek
Pitcher, 1941–1953

Steve Gromek, originally an infielder, became a pitcher after tearing a shoulder muscle in the minors. The lanky right–hander learned to throw sidearm, and the new delivery made his pitches hard to hit. He won 19 games in 1945, but the Indians soon sent him to the bullpen, from where he would make his lasting contribution. In relief, he was a vital part of the 1948 championship team. Named to start Game 4 of the World Series, Gromek threw a complete game and beat the Boston Braves, 2–1. Gromek was traded to Detroit in 1953 and again made a starter. Gromek notched 18 wins for the fifth–place Tigers in 1954.

Bob Feller and Frankie Hayes
Yankee Stadium, 1946

When 27-year old Bob Feller returned from World War II after almost four years, questions surrounded him: Was he still the same pitcher? Did he possess the same overpowering fastball?

On April 30, 1946, Cleveland fans got their answers. Facing the powerhouse Yankees in New York, Feller threw a no-hitter to defeat the "Bronx Bombers," 1–0. The game's only run came on a ninth-inning home run by Feller's battery mate, catcher Frankie Hayes. Feller went on to dominate the American League in 1946, with 26 wins, 10 shutouts and 348 strikeouts.

The patch shown on Hayes' left sleeve was worn by the 1946 Indians to commemorate the 150th anniversary of the City of Cleveland.

Bill Veeck
Owner, 1946–1949

Is it possible that any other owner had a more immediate impact on their new team and city than Bill Veeck? Long before he gained fame for sending a midget, Eddie Gaedel, up to the plate to bat for the St. Louis Browns, Veeck gave Cleveland a championship team, ending a 27-year drought.

Veeck spent his entire life around ballparks, learning the business from his father, who ran the Chicago Cubs for parts of two decades. In 1941, Veeck struck out on his own and purchased the minor league club in Milwaukee. He scheduled games at 11 a.m. so that wartime shift workers could attend. And he spent hours at the front gate greeting fans and soliciting ideas on how to improve his last-place team. The fans ate it up.

In June 1946, Veeck sold the Milwaukee franchise for a chance to make his mark in the majors. When he heard the Cleveland team was for sale, he sneaked into town and spent a week talking to bartenders and cabdrivers about the team. He became convinced that Cleveland could again become a great baseball town. He put together a dozen investors, including comedian Bob Hope, and purchased the club.

As he did in the minors, Veeck began staging outrageous promotions. Ladies arriving at the stadium were presented with live orchids, flown in from Hawaii. Players and fans were treated to live music and wrestling matches before and after games. During the offseason, Veeck spent his free time speaking to civic groups around Cleveland. He often addressed more than 200 groups in a year.

But it was his ability to scout baseball talent that paid the biggest dividends for the Indians. Veeck made trades, acquired talent he had seen in the minors and assembled the pieces of a championship team. His signing of Larry Doby as the American League's first black player was a risky move and raised eyebrows around the league. But Cleveland fans loved Veeck's daring and fan-friendly style and responded with record-setting attendance. In 1948, 2.6 million fans would crowd Municipal Stadium, setting a single-season mark that stood until 1995 and the arrival of Jacobs Field.

Veeck owned the Indians just three seasons. A baseball gypsy, he later owned the St. Louis Browns and the Chicago White Sox, twice. Veeck died in 1986. He was elected to the Hall of Fame in 1991.

Jim Hegan
Catcher, 1941–42; 1946–57

For more than a decade, Jim Hegan was the glue that held together the Indians' vaunted pitching staff, proving that the value of a catcher is measured beyond his batting average. Hegan was a five–time All–Star although he never hit over .250 in any of 10 seasons as the everyday catcher. Hegan was behind the plate for three no–hitters: Don Black's in 1947, Bob Lemon's in 1948 and Bob Feller's in 1951. Hegan's knowledge of opposing hitters certified him as one of the league's best signal–callers. Red Sox great Ted Williams once said, "I'm one hit better when Hegan is out of the lineup."

When his playing days were over, Hegan spent nearly 20 years as a coach with the Yankees and the Tigers. He died in 1984 at age 63.

Don Black
Pitcher, 1946–1948

Don Black's career was marred by tragedy. His constant drinking got him released by the Athletics in 1945. Cleveland decided to take a chance on him. They sent Black to the minors, where he continued to drink and lose. Indians owner Bill Veeck summoned Black to Cleveland and gave him a choice. If he'd join Alcoholics Anonymous, Veeck would pay off his creditors. Black agreed and good things began to happen. During the offseason, Veeck got Black a job with a Cleveland company so that he could attend his weekly meetings. The next season, Black threw a no–hitter and won 10 games for the Indians. But his success was short–lived.

On September 13, 1948, while batting against the Browns in a game at Municipal Stadium, Black collapsed to the ground. He had suffered a brain hemorrhage. His pitching career was over. The Indians staged a benefit 10 days later and raised more than $40,000 for Black. He was given a full share of the team's 1948 World Series winnings and Veeck later paid him his entire 1949 salary.

Black's hard luck continued in 1957, when he was seriously injured in a car accident. He died two years later at the age of 42, while watching his former team on television.

Bill Veeck and Larry Doby
Comiskey Park, Chicago, 1947

On July 5, 1947, Indians owner Bill Veeck signed 23–year–old infielder Larry Doby as the first black player in the American League, only 10 weeks after Jackie Robinson debuted with the Brooklyn Dodgers. Doby had been a four–sport standout at East Side High in Patterson, N. J. Later, playing with the Newark Eagles of the Negro Leagues, he caught the attention of Abe Saperstein, owner of the legendary Harlem Globetrotters, who recommended him to Veeck.

Veeck sent his chief scout to look Doby over. The scout's report contained two words: Buy him. Veeck phoned the owner of the Newark club, Mrs. Effa Manley, to negotiate a sale. Mrs. Manley agreed to sell Doby's contract for $15,000, but only after assurances that her star player would get a raise over the $4,000 he was making with Newark. Doby caught a train to Chicago the next day and joined the Indians.

Dale Mitchell
Outfielder, 1946–1956

Dale Mitchell was a fixture in left field during the Indians' golden era of the late 1940s and early 1950s. A career .312 hitter, he was exceptionally fast and one of the league's best lead–off hitters. Mitchell struck out just 119 times in almost 4,000 major league at–bats. In 1949, he led the league in hits and triples. In an era of great outfielders, Mitchell was named to the All–Star team three times.

But by 1954, Mitchell was being used as a pinch hitter. He was traded in 1956 to Brooklyn, where he is best remembered for making the final out of Don Larsen's perfect game of the 1956 World Series. Mitchell returned to Oklahoma the next year and worked in the oil business. He later became president of a cement company. He died in 1987 of a heart attack at age 65.

Bob Hope
Municipal Stadium. 1947

Bob Hope was one of a dozen investors who bought the Indians with Bill Veeck. Hope was raised in Cleveland but had long since moved away. Prior to the first night game of 1947, Hope made a surprise appearance before the crowd of 61,000. Donning an Indians cap, Hope clowned in the dugout with Indians manager Lou Boudreau and his coaches. Ownership of baseball teams apparently appealed to the Hollywood crowd. Hope's movie partner, Bing Crosby, was a minority owner of the Pittsburgh Pirates at the same time.

Joe Gordon
Second baseman, 1947-1950
Manager, 1958–1960

Second baseman Joe Gordon teamed with shortstop Lou Boudreau to give the Indians the finest infield tandem in the league during the late 1940s. A graceful fielder, Gordon came from New York, where he was a six–time All–Star and the league MVP in 1942. But when he feuded with Yankee General Manager Larry MacPhail, he was dealt to Cleveland for pitcher Allie Reynolds.

Gordon showed unusual power for an infielder. He hit 32 home runs and drove in 124 RBIs during Cleveland's 1948 championship season. Gordon left the Indians after the 1950 season to spend two years managing in Sacramento. In 1958, he returned to manage the Indians and led the team to a second–place finish in 1959. But Gordon didn't get along with newly–arrived General Manager Frank Lane. The next year, in one of the strangest trades in Indian history, Lane traded Gordon to the Detroit Tigers for their manager, Jimmy Dykes. It was the major league's first and only swap of managers.

Gene Bearden
Pitcher, 1947–1950

For one brief moment in 1948, Gene Bearden was the talk of the American League. During the season, Bearden, a knuckleballer, won 20 games, threw six shutouts and led the league with a 2.43 ERA. Indians manager Lou Boudreau played a hunch and chose the tall left–hander to start the one–game playoff against the Red Sox, a game that would decide the 1948 pennant. Bearden held Boston to five hits and the Indians won, 8–3.

In the World Series, Bearden won Game 3 by blanking the Boston Braves, 2–0. Later, he saved Game 6 to help bring the title to Cleveland. But 1948 was Bearden's last winning season. Yankee manager Casey Stengal, who'd seen Bearden pitch in the Pacific Coast League, told his hitters to lay off Bearden's knuckleball because it moved out of the strike zone. The result was Bearden started walking batters, became ineffective, and was soon traded. He played with four more teams in three years before retiring.

Jimmy Dudley and Jack Graney
Municipal Stadium, 1948

In 1948, two of the greatest names in Cleveland broadcast history worked together for the first time. Veteran Jack Graney began broadcasting Indians games on the radio in 1932. His 14 seasons as an Indian outfielder gave him instant credibility and his direct no–nonsense delivery set a standard widely copied by others. He summed up his philosophy recalling, "I just try to follow the ball and leave fancy words to the others." Graney retired from the radio booth after the 1953 season.

Jimmy Dudley spent three years at a Chicago station before arriving in Cleveland. In 1947, behind the mike for an amateur game at Municipal Stadium, Dudley got noticed by the president of a local brewery that had just purchased the radio rights to the Indians' games. Dudley was hired and his smooth Virginia cadence was an instant hit with listeners. The 1948 championship season, his first, was the high point of his career.

Dudley spent the next 20 seasons calling some of the Tribe's leanest seasons, but he remained the eternal optimist, recalling, "I never saw a bad game, only a few long ones and a few slow ones." Dudley was fired after the 1967 season and replaced by Herb Score. In 1997, Dudley was awarded the Ford Frick Award by the Hall of Fame for his career in broadcasting.

Leroy "Satchel" Paige
Pitcher, 1948–1949

When "Satchel" Paige arrived in Cleveland in July 1948, the press was sure that his signing represented another Bill Veeck publicity stunt. Paige was at least 42 years old, quite possibly as old as 48, but no one knew for sure and Paige liked it that way. The press questioned his age, his ability to pitch, and whether Paige thought he could strike out major league hitters, all of whom happened to be white. Even the editor of *The Sporting News* railed against the move, writing, "To bring in a pitching rookie of Paige's age is to demean the standards of baseball."

Paige had been the dominant pitcher in the Negro Leagues for more than 20 years. He was the league's best gate attraction; a master showman on and off the mound. The flamboyant Paige relied on a variety of trick pitches he called his "bat dodger," "jump ball" and "nothin' ball," as well as two speeds of fastball he nicknamed "long Tom" and "short Tom." His control was exceptional.

Cleveland fans showed up in record numbers to see the ageless Paige baffle American League hitters. When Paige went 6–1 over the final three months of the season, he countered his critics, "I demeaned the big leagues considerably. I win six and lose one."

Ken Keltner
Spring training, 1948

Third baseman Ken Keltner is the man responsible for stopping Joe DiMaggio's 56–game hitting streak in 1941. When the Yankees visited Cleveland in July, DiMaggio's streak stood at 55 games. In the first game of the series, on July 16, DiMaggio had three hits. The next night, his fortunes changed before a crowd of 67,468 at Municipal Stadium. In the first inning, DiMaggio hit a low curve ball over the third base bag. Keltner backhanded the ball and threw out DiMaggio at first. In his second at bat, DiMaggio walked. In the seventh inning, the Yankee Clipper hit another shot over the third base bag. Keltner made a backhanded stab that propelled him into foul territory, and his long throw beat DiMaggio to first by a step.

In the eighth, DiMaggio grounded into a double play to complete his 0–for–4 night. The hitting streak was over at 56 games. The next day, playing across town at League Park, DiMaggio got two hits to start another streak that would ultimately stretch to 16 games.

Later in life, Keltner recalled the plays matter of factly. "The first time he was up, I played him deep because he never bunted. I played him close to the line because if he hits one down the line, it's a double. It just wasn't Joe's night. He hit the ball hard enough, but they just weren't there."

Satchel Paige and Bob Feller
Municipal Stadium, 1948

Long before he joined the Indians, Satchel Paige spent two decades barnstorming with Negro League teams and pitching exhibition games against white major leaguers. In 1934, Paige outdueled the legendary Dizzy Dean for 13 innings, winning 1–0. Cleveland pitching ace Bob Feller knew Paige from the barnstorming circuit. In 1946, Feller had put together a team of major league all–stars to face the Satchel Paige All–Stars on a month–long exhibition tour covering 17 states.

When Bill Veeck sold the Indians after the 1949 season, Paige was released. He re–signed with Veeck two years later in St. Louis and won 12 games in 1952 for the seventh–place team. Paige's final major–league appearance was in 1965 for Charley Finley's Kansas City Athletics, where he pitched three scoreless innings. Paige was believed to be 59 at the time. Elected to the Hall of Fame in 1971, Paige died in Kansas City in 1982.

**Orestes "Minnie" Minoso
Outfielder, 1949; 1951;
1958–1959**

Minoso was one of the first
modern-day Cuban players to
succeed in the major leagues.
Before the arrival of Washington's
Pedro Ramos and Camilo Pasqual,
there was Minoso, dubbed the
"Cuban Comet" for his speed.

Minoso led the league in stolen
bases his first three full seasons in
the majors. Opposing pitchers
threw at him to try to intimidate
him. Ten times he would lead the
league in number of times hit by
a pitch.

Early in the 1951 season, the
Indians traded Minoso to the
White Sox. It was a major blunder.
The next year, he was chosen *The
Sporting News'* Rookie of the Year
for hitting .325 and leading the
league in triples.

A seven-time All-Star, Minoso
would re-join the Indians in 1958
for two seasons, hitting .302 and
adding 45 home runs. He was
traded back to the White Sox
after the 1960 season. He later
came out of retirement in 1978
and again in 1980, allowing him
to claim the distinction of playing
in five decades.

Al Rosen
Third baseman, 1947–1956

Al Rosen emerged as the Indians' everyday third baseman in 1950, replacing Ken Keltner and becoming the premier power–hitting third sacker in the majors. Nicknamed "Flip" for his motion as a softball pitcher, Rosen was a four–sport star in his native Miami. He was also an amateur boxer who had his nose broken 11 times, although only once in the ring. Most of the others occurred on the ballfield. In 1950, Rosen led the league with 37 home runs. He drove in 100 runs for five consecutive years. During the 1954 All–Star game, played before his hometown fans at Municipal

Stadium, Rosen hit two homers and drove in five runs.

But in the offseason, Rosen suffered whiplash in an auto accident and during the 1955 season, his power numbers declined. A second sub–par season led to booing by Indians fans. Rosen reacted by retiring after the 1956 season and beginning what would become a successful career as a stockbroker. In 1978, Rosen returned to baseball as an executive with the New York Yankees. He later was general manager with the Astros and Giants.

Bill Veeck and Lou Boudreau
Shibe Park, 1949

Six months after this picture was taken, owner Bill Veeck and shortstop/manager Lou Boudreau would be gone from Cleveland. Veeck decided to sell the team in November 1949 to pay his divorce settlement and because after three years, he felt he'd done all he could do for the franchise. The sale began to define Veeck as a turnaround artist who bought floundering franchises, made them successful quickly and then moved on. Boudreau was released after the 1949 season, having played out a two–year contract he'd gotten from Veeck after Indians fans came to his aid.

A showdown between the two men erupted after the 1947 season when Veeck went to New York for the World Series between the Yankees and Dodgers. Holding court in his favorite booth at the legendary Toots Shor's restaurant, Veeck told the assembled sportswriters about a trade proposal he'd received. The St. Louis Browns were offering to trade shortstop Vern Stephens for Boudreau in a multi–player deal. Veeck liked Boudreau as a player, but not as a manager. He was intrigued that Stephens was three years younger than Boudreau and had nearly identical power stats. Veeck wanted to know the sportswriters' opinions of the offer, but cautioned them that the entire conversation was "off the record" and not for publication.

However, a Chicago columnist printed details of the proposed trade a few days later and all hell broke loose back in Cleveland. Fans were outraged. Who did Veeck think he was to even consider trading their idol? Veeck knew a public relations blunder when he saw one, and immediately flew home to Cleveland to placate Indians fans. Only when St. Louis withdrew the offer, was the matter put to rest. Veeck then quieted the fans by signing his manager to a two–year contract. Boudreau, feeling the pressure to produce, responded with the best year of his career in 1948. He led the Indians to the pennant.

Larry Doby
Outfielder, 1947–1955; 1958

After the 1947 season, shortstop Larry Doby was taken aside by the Indians coaches and told to prepare to become a major league outfielder. Hall of Fame outfielder Tris Speaker became Doby's personal instructor the next spring, hitting hundreds of fly balls to his outfield student. The result was that by 1950, *The Sporting News* recognized Doby as the top center fielder in the majors, ahead of New York's Joe DiMaggio and Brooklyn's Duke Snider. He was also selected for that year's All–Star game, the first of seven straight. In 1954, Doby led the league in home runs (32) and RBIs (126), but finished second to Yogi Berra as league MVP.

The Indians traded Doby to the White Sox after the 1955 season, but he returned to Cleveland for one final season in 1958. Beginning in 1971, Doby spent five seasons as a coach with the Expos and Indians before becoming the major league's second black manager, with the White Sox, in 1978. In 1994, the Indians retired Doby's number 14 and, in 1998, he was elected to the Hall of Fame.

Luke Easter
Spring training, 1950

Luke Easter spent five seasons in the Negro Leagues before attracting the attention of major league scouts. He was a giant of a man known for long–distance home runs. He was once turned down for a tryout by the Chicago American Giants of the Negro leagues because he was deemed "too big" to play. In 1947, he replaced the legendary Josh Gibson as the first baseman for the barnstorming Homestead Grays. In 1948, Easter became the only man to ever hit a ball into the center field bleachers of New York's Polo Grounds, a mammoth shot estimated at more than 500 feet.

Signed by Bill Veeck, Easter arrived in Cleveland in 1949 after tearing up the Pacific Coast League for San Diego, where he hit .363 and drove in 92 runs in 80 games. However, Easter was not an immediate fan favorite in Cleveland. Forced to share time with veteran Mickey Vernon at first base, Easter got off to a slow start and was repeatedly booed by Indians fans. Despite a series of leg injuries and two weak ankles broken in an auto accident, Easter twice drove in more than 100 runs for the Tribe. In 1950, he hit the longest home run ever recorded at Municipal Stadium, a shot into the upper right–field deck that measured 447 feet.

Hank Greenberg and Ellis Ryan
1951

Former Tiger great Hank Greenberg joined Bill Veeck in 1948 as a minority owner and vice–president of the Indians. Greenberg helped coach some of the younger Indians players and assisted Veeck by evaluating trade proposals.

When Veeck sold the club after the 1949 season, Ellis Ryan became team president and Greenberg became general manager. Ryan left after the 1952 season, leaving Greenberg in charge until 1957. In 1959, Greenberg re–joined Veeck in Chicago for five years as vice president of the White Sox.

Mickey Vernon
First baseman, 1949–1950; 1958

Mickey Vernon was a part of one of the most lopsided trades in Indians history, pulled off by Bill Veeck at the 1948 winter meetings. In a deal with the Washington Senators, Veeck gave up three mediocre players for pitcher Early Wynn and Vernon, who had won the 1946 American League batting title. Vernon was also a superb defensive first baseman.

However, when Veeck left the Indians and Hank Greenberg became the team's general manager, Greenberg decided to trade Vernon back to Washington to make room for Luke Easter. Back in Washington, Vernon would win a second batting title in 1953 and lead the league in doubles for two straight years.

When the Indians finally re-acquired him, Vernon had one good season left and was an All-Star in 1958. He retired after the 1960 season with 2,495 career hits.

Mike Garcia
Pitcher, 1948–1959

Edward Miguel Garcia was a key member of the most dominant pitching rotation in Indians history, along with Bob Lemon, Early Wynn and Bob Feller. Nicknamed "the Big Bear," Garcia was twice a 20–game winner for the Tribe. Mixing an overpowering fastball with a deceptive slider, he twice led the league in shutouts. In 1954, when the Indians won the AL pennant, Garcia won 19 games and led the league with a 2.64 ERA. He lost his only World Series start to the New York Giants, who swept the Indians in four straight games.

After winning 138 games in nine years for the Indians, Garcia slipped and injured his back on a wet field in spring training in 1958. He suffered a slipped disc, effectively ending his career. Garcia retired during the 1961 season and operated a dry cleaning business in Parma, Ohio. In the 1970s, he began suffering from diabetes and kidney failure and was forced to sell the business to pay his medical bills. Garcia died in 1986 at age 62.

Luke Easter
First baseman, 1949–1954

Luke Easter got a late start in the majors at age 34, and although he hit 86 home runs in his first three full seasons with the Indians, his major league career was all but over after four years.

Slowed by repeated leg injuries, Easter was sent back to the minors where he spent another 10 seasons. Easter became a cult hero in Buffalo and Rochester, continuing to amaze fans with his mammoth home runs. He played his last game in 1964 at age 48.

In 1967, Easter returned to Cleveland to work at the TRW aircraft plant. By 1979, he was in charge of the employee payroll, which required him to carry large sums of cash to and from the bank. On March 29, 1979, Easter was shot and killed by two men as he left the bank with more than $40,000 in cash. At the funeral home, more than 4,000 people paid their respects.

Early Wynn
Pitcher, 1949–1957; 1963

Early Wynn pitched in the major leagues for eight years before he learned to throw a curve ball. Wynn had been a consistent winner in Washington, relying almost exclusively on his fastball. But when Indians pitching coach Mel Harder taught Wynn to throw the curve and his career really took off. Armed with his new pitch, Wynn became one of the most dominant pitchers in the majors. He won at least 20 games four times and became the workhorse of the Indians' staff. Twice, he led the league in innings pitched. During the 1950s, he had more strikeouts than any other pitcher. Wynn was famous for his intimidating demeanor on the mound. Mickey Mantle once said Wynn was "so mean he'd knock you down in the dugout."

Wynn was also an excellent hitter and was often asked to pinch hit. But when he had his first losing season for the Tribe in 1957, Wynn was traded to the White Sox. There, he rebounded to have the best year of his career in 1959, notching 22 victories and winning the Cy Young award. Released by Chicago after the 1962 season, he returned to Cleveland to pitch and win the 300th, and final, game of his career. In 1972, Wynn was elected to the Hall of Fame.

Al Lopez
Manager, 1951–1956

When Manager Lou Boudreau was released after the 1950 season, the Indians had the perfect replacement in mind: Al Lopez, who for three years had been managing the Indians' top farm club at Indianapolis, finishing first once and second twice. Bill Veeck tried to make Lopez the Indians manager in 1948, but his attempted trade of Boudreau to the Browns backfired (see page 107).

Because of his experience during 19 years as a major-league catcher, Lopez came to be known as a player's manager. His easy-going style was especially effective in handling the Indians pitching staff.

During five of his six years in Cleveland, the Indians finished second to the hated Yankees. But in 1954, Lopez guided the Indians to the World Series against the New York Giants. However, the Giants swept the series in four straight games. Lopez dryly answered his critics. "They say anything can happen in a short series," he said. "I just didn't expect it to be that short."

Lopez resigned after the 1956 season, but was immediately signed by Bill Veeck to manage the Chicago White Sox. Lopez led the White Sox to a pennant in 1959. In 1977, Lopez was inducted into the Hall of Fame.

Ray Boone
Shortstop, 1948–1953

Ray Boone, who begat a baseball family dynasty, was groomed to take over for Lou Boudreau as the Indians' shortstop. There was only one problem with that. Boone had been a catcher in the minors and had chronically bad knees, which limited his range in the field. Cleveland fans were spoiled by Boudreau. They expected their shortstop to hit well over .300 and be a wizard with the glove. Boone could do neither. He freely admitted the fan's reaction bothered him.

Early in the 1953 season, Boone was traded to Detroit. Switched to third base, where range wasn't an issue, he relaxed and developed as one of the league's steadiest performers. His son, Bob, and grandsons, Bret and Aaron, would all play in the majors.

Bobby Avila
Second baseman, 1949–1958

Bobby Avila was the first Mexican player to succeed in the major leagues. Spending his first two years in Cleveland on the bench, he learned the strengths of opposing players and learned English from his roommate, pitcher Mike Garcia. When he finally replaced Joe Gordon as the Indians' everyday second baseman in 1951, Avila quickly impressed his teammates by batting .304. In 1952, he led the league in triples, but saved his best for the Indians' 1954 championship season. Avila batted .341 that year, winning the AL batting crown and becoming a national hero in his homeland.

Traded by Cleveland after the 1958 season, he eventually returned to Mexico and spent several years as a club owner and president of the Mexican League. He was later elected mayor of Veracruz.

Al Smith
Outfielder, 1953–1957

Al Smith could play several positions well. Speed was his greatest asset and in 1954, he became the regular left fielder. He had his best year in 1955, when he led the league in runs scored, averaged .306 and hit 22 home runs. Nicknamed "Fuzzy" because of his heavy beard, Smith was traded to the White Sox along with pitcher Early Wynn for Minnie Minoso after the 1957 season. There, he won a second pennant with the White Sox in 1959.

Harry "Suitcase" Simpson
Outfielder, 1951–1955

Harry Simpson earned the nickname "Suitcase" because he was constantly being traded. He played for 17 teams over his 11 years in the major and minor leagues. A superb defensive outfielder, Simpson never hit well enough to claim an everyday slot with the Indians. His best season came in 1956 with the Kansas City Athletics, when he hit 21 home runs and drove in 105 runs. He died in 1979 in Akron, Ohio.

Ray Narleski, Don Mossi and Hal Newhouser
1954 Bullpen

The 1954 Indians were a juggernaut, winning 111 games and finishing eight games ahead of the Yankees. The batters led the league with 156 home runs and the pitching staff had a league best 2.78 ERA. But it was the work of the bullpen that nailed down the victories. Manager Al Lopez used his bullpen interchangeably. Ray Narleski had 13 saves and a 2.22 ERA. Don Mossi, nicknamed "the Sphinx" because of his large ears, had seven saves, a 1.94 ERA and went 6–1. Hal Newhouser, a future Hall of Famer, finished up his career with seven saves and a 7–2 record. Unfortunately, this trio couldn't help the Indians avoid being swept in four games by the Giants in the 1954 World Series.

Art Houtteman
Pitcher, 1953–1957

Art Houtteman was the major pitching surprise of the Indians' 1954 championship season. Houtteman came from the Detroit Tigers the year before, where he had won 34 games over two seasons. But Detroit let him go after he returned from a year's hitch in the military and won just eight games in 1952. Cleveland traded Ray Boone, Steve Gromek and two other players to Detroit for Houtteman and three mediocre players. The big payoff came in 1954 when Houtteman went 15–7 to help the Indians win a record 111 games. The following year, he was used primarily as a reliever. Houtteman retired after the 1957 season at age 30.

Vic Wertz
First baseman, 1954–1958

Vic Wertz made one of the most famous outs in World Series history. He hit the drive to deep center field that Giants' outfielder Willie Mays caught over his shoulder in Game 1 of the 1954 Series. With two Indians on base, Mays' basket catch saved two runs and kept the game tied. The Giants eventually won in 10 innings, despite four hits by Wertz, the Indians' best hitter in the Series. Wertz later recalled, "Mays' catch was the psychological crusher. We never recovered."

In 1955, Wertz was stricken with polio in mid–season, but completely recovered. He had one of his finest seasons in 1956, when he hit 32 home runs and drove in 106 runs. He had 29 homers and 105 RBIs the following year. A leg injury in 1958 caused the Indians to trade him to the Red Sox.

Wertz retired after the 1963 season with 266 career home runs. He settled in Detroit and operated a successful beer distributorship for 20 years until his death in 1983.

Bob Lemon
Pitcher, 1946–1958

Bob Lemon was the most consistent winner during the glory years of the great Indians' pitching staff. He was a 20–game winner seven times and liked to finish what he started, leading the league in complete games five times. Ted Williams said Lemon was "one of the three toughest pitchers I ever faced."

Lemon was a seven–time All–Star and an excellent hitter, belting 37 career home runs. In the 1948 World Series, he won Games 2 and 6, allowing the Boston Braves two runs over 16 innings. In the 1954 Series, he lost Game 1 when he gave up a home run to the Giant's Dusty Rhodes in the bottom of the tenth inning.

Lemon retired after the 1958 season and began a career as a coach, scout and manager with several clubs. He managed the Kansas City Royals for three years and the White Sox for two. Lemon twice managed the New York Yankees and, with them, won the World Series in 1978. Lemon was elected to the Hall of Fame in 1976. The Indians retired his number, 21, in 1998. He died in 2000.

Al Lopez, Mike Garcia, Bob Lemon, Early Wynn
Yankee Stadium, 1954

Between 1951 and 1956, Manager Al Lopez saw his "Big 3" pitchers win 342 games for Cleveland. This trio's dominance over American League hitters led the Indians to the pennant in 1954 and a heated rivalry with the New York Yankees.

Al Rosen
MVP Award Ceremony, 1954

Indians third baseman Al Rosen had a
monster year in 1953. He batted .336 and
led the league with 43 home runs and
145 RBIs. Rosen missed winning the Triple
Crown because Washington's Mickey
Vernon batted .337. The title wasn't
decided until Rosen's final at bat of the
season's final game. He got three hits in
his first three trips to the plate, but on
the fourth, he was called out on a close
play at first.

The following July, he was presented
with the American League MVP award.
Rosen is shown here receiving the award
from *Cleveland News* sportswriter Ed
McAuley, who was the national chairman
of the Baseball Writer's Association.

Ferris Fain
First baseman, 1955

Ferris Fain was a two–time batting champion with the Philadelphia Athletics and considered one of the finest fielding first baseman of his era. But by the time he arrived in Cleveland, his career was all but over. Fain would play just 56 games for the Indians before bad knees forced him to retire at age 34.

Ralph Kiner
Outfielder, 1955

Ralph Kiner won seven consecutive National League home–run titles with the Pittsburgh Pirates. In 1955, his former roommate in Pittsburgh, Indians GM Hank Greenberg, sent $60,000 and two players to the Pirates to bring Kiner's booming bat to Cleveland. But Kiner was on the downhill part of his career. He wound up having a bad back and hit just 18 home runs in 1955. He retired at age 32 after one year in Cleveland.

In 1962, Kiner began a second career in broadcasting. He spent the next four decades calling New York Mets games. Kiner was elected to the Hall of Fame in 1975.

Bob Feller
Municipal Stadium, 1956

By 1955, Bob Feller was no longer pitching every four days. He spent most of his time in the bullpen, only occasionally starting a game for the Indians.

After 266 victories and 18 years in the majors, Feller hung up his number 19 jersey for the final time after the 1956 season. In 1957, his uniform number was the first to be retired by the Indians.

The three and a half years he spent in the military at the height of his career almost certainly cost him the coveted goal of 300 wins. Feller was elected to the Hall of Fame in 1962. He remains the Indians' all–time leader in wins, strike–outs and innings pitched.

Herb Score
Pitcher, 1955–1959

Herb Score was going to be the next Bob Feller. In his first season, he won 16 games, led the league with 245 strike-outs and was named Rookie of the Year. The next year, he notched 20 wins, threw five shutouts and struck out 263 batters in 249 innings. Never before had a rookie pitcher thrown more than 200 innings and averaged more than one strikeout per inning in his first two years.

After two seasons with the Indians, *The Sporting News* speculated that Score would become the greatest left-handed pitcher of all time. Teammate Rocky Colavito said, "He made perfect seem second rate." Armed with an overpowering fastball and a tremendous curveball, Score was set to re-write the record books. But in 1957, all that changed.

On May 7, Score started against the Yankees at Municipal Stadium. The second batter up was shortstop Gil McDougald. McDougald hit a sharp line drive that caught Score flush in the face, breaking his nose. Carried off the field by his teammates, Score was blinded in his left eye. Eventually his eyesight returned, but Score missed the rest of the 1957 season.

Over the years, a myth developed that this freak injury ended Score's career. Score later set the record straight, recalling, "the McDougald line drive had nothing to do with my career ending prematurely. I came back in '58 throwing as hard as ever. I had 48 strike-outs in 41 innings. Physically, I was never better. I was pitching in Washington on a cold, rainy night. Late in the game, I felt a pain in my elbow. I was diagnosed as having a tendon injury. I laid off and came back about three weeks later. I went in as a reliever and ended the game on a pop-up. But I hurt my arm again on that pitch. After that pitch, I was never the same again."

Score spent parts of another four seasons in the majors. He even returned to the minors briefly, but it was never the same. Score retired after the 1962 season. In 1964, he began a new career broadcasting Indians games, spending more than 30 years behind the microphone.

Rocky Colavito
Outfielder, 1955–1959

Rocky Colavito wanted to be Joe DiMaggio. Growing up in the shadows of Yankee Stadium, young Rocco, his given name, was the son of Italian immigrants. He patterned his batting stance and grip after his boyhood hero. When he was signed by the Indians and sent to the minors in 1950, he even requested DiMaggio's number five for his jersey. When he struggled as a hitter, his coach persuaded Colavito to drop the DiMaggio impersonation. A new stance and a new grip soon produced a big increase in Colavito's power numbers.

By 1956, his matinee idol looks and exceptionally strong arm made him the most popular athlete in Cleveland. Colavito would hang around the stadium for hours after the game to sign autographs for his adoring fans, many of them young women. His home run totals increased every year until he tied for the league-lead with 42 in 1959. That year, he hit four home runs in a game at Baltimore and was named to the All-Star team.

But Colavito was prone to batting slumps. When fans squawked about his lapses at the plate, a local sportswriter coined the slogan, "Don't Knock the Rock" and it started a rallying cry for Colavito's loyal fans. Colavito helped the Indians finish in second place in 1959. Cleveland fans had no way of knowing it would be another 35 years before the team would reach those heights again.

Roger Maris
Outfielder, 1957–1958

Roger Maris is the one that got away from the Cleveland Indians. Signed for $15,000 out of high school, Maris rose quickly through the Indians' minor league ranks. On Opening Day 1957, Maris was the starting left fielder for the Indians. He went 3–for–5 in his first game. The next day, he hit his first of 14 home runs that season, a grand slam. But Maris only knew one style of play–all out. He jammed his wrist running into the outfield wall and suffered a series of nagging injuries that kept his batting average below .250 for most of the year. When the season ended, Indians General Manager Frank Lane asked Maris to play winter ball in the Dominican Republic for $1,000 a month. Maris thought the pay too low and refused. Instead, he returned to Fargo, N.D., and worked at a radio station as a sportscaster. Lane later said, "I guess you could say we never got along after that."

In 1958, the Kansas City Athletics called Lane to ask about a trade. They were interested in Colavito, but Lane told them he was too popular with the fans. He suggested Maris instead. On June 15, the trade was announced.

Two years later, Maris won the first of two consecutive MVP awards. In 1961, he broke Babe Ruth's single–season home–run record of 60.

Alfonso "Chico" Carrasquel
Shortstop, 1956–1958

In 1956, the Indians traded 33–year–old outfielder Larry Doby to the Chicago White Sox for Chico Carrasquel, a four–time All–Star and one of the American League's premier defensive shortstops. Carrasquel became the Tribe's best shortstop since Lou Boudreau. But early in 1958, he was traded to Kansas City. He retired after the 1959 season at age 31, returning to Venezuela a national hero.

Hoyt Wilhelm
Pitcher, 1957–1958

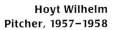

James Hoyt Wilhelm made 263 consecutive appearances as a relief pitcher before being sold to Cleveland late in 1957. The next year, Indians Manager Bobby Bragan decided to make Wilhelm a starting pitcher. The results were mixed and by August, Cleveland had given up on Wilhelm and waived him. One month later, with the Orioles, Wilhelm threw a no–hitter against the Yankees. His trademark pitch was the knuckleball, which put so little strain on his arm that he would spend another 14 seasons in the majors and record 227 career saves. In 1985, Wilhelm was the first relief pitcher inducted into the Hall of Fame.

Rocky Colavito and Harvey Kuenn
Municipal Stadium, 1960

Two days before the start of the 1960 season, Indians fans woke up to find their favorite player gone. Slugger Rocky Colavito had been traded to the Detroit Tigers for Harvey Kuenn, a six–time All–Star who had won the league batting title in 1959. Kuenn hit for a high average, but he was no Colavito. Indians general manager Frank Lane, who believed home runs were overrated, tried to assure fans. "I say I swapped a hamburger for a steak," he proclaimed.

Colavito continued his slugging in Detroit, hitting 149 home runs in four seasons. Kuenn batted .308 for the Indians, but was traded to the Giants after one season.

Frank Lane
Executive, 1957–1960

Four decades after he stepped down in Cleveland, Frank Lane's name still elicits howls from loyal Indians fans. Nicknamed "Trader Lane" for constantly swapping players, Lane was a flamboyant self–promoter who learned his trade in front office jobs with the White Sox and Cardinals. Named general manager in 1957, Lane claimed to hold the solution for rebuilding the Cleveland franchise.

Lane started by guaranteeing that attendance would top one million in his first season, a projected increase of almost 35 percent. Then he went to work justifying his nickname, making 51 trades covering 118 players in three years. He dealt away prospects and veterans alike. Lane even made the only trade of managers in major league history, swapping the Indians' Joe Gordon to Detroit for Jimmy Dykes. The Indians finished second in 1959, but Lane continued to tinker. He was openly critical of players, and often took a position in the stands to yell insults at offending players.

It was Lane's trading of Rocky Colavito to the Tigers in 1960 that cemented his unsavory reputation in Cleveland sports history. Fans took to the streets to protest the departure of their hero. Lane was hanged in effigy from city windows. Fans staged a mock funeral procession to the ballpark and threatened to boycott home games. Lane remained steadfast, proclaiming, "We did it because we think it will help us win the pennant."

After three tumultuous years, Lane left Cleveland to work for Charley Finley, the eccentric owner of the Kansas City Athletics. But their two egos clashed and Lane was gone within a year. He later ran the NBA franchise in Chicago. His last position in baseball was with the Milwaukee Brewers in the early 1970s. Lane died in 1981 at age 85.

Jimmy Piersall
Outfielder, 1959–1961

Jimmy Piersall was a talented outfielder known for his outrageous behavior on and off the field. He argued with umpires. He threw tantrums on the field. And when he hit his 100th home run, he ran the bases backwards. His second year in the majors, with the Red Sox, Piersall had problems with his nerves and spent time in a psychiatric hospital. Later, he publicly proclaimed, "I'm crazy and I have the papers to prove it."

Piersall's hustling style and on–field antics made him a fan favorite, but he was traded to Washington following the 1961 season. He later became a broadcaster in Chicago, where his outspoken style continued to make headlines.

Vic Power
First baseman, 1958–1961

Vic Power was the first black player signed by the New York Yankees. Sent to the minors, his dating of white women got him labeled an "unsavory character" and the Yankees traded him to the Philadelphia Athletics rather than call him up as their first black player.

Power, who was from Puerto Rico and spoke broken English that sometimes left him misunderstood by the media, had a brash style that made him a frequent target of bean balls. A winner of seven Gold Gloves, he was considered the flashiest first baseman of his day. But Power's signature move of fielding everything one-handed got him branded a "showboat." He was a notorious bad-ball hitter and adopted an unorthodox batting stance, leading Yankee pitcher Whitey Ford to proclaim, "Power is the only hitter I know whose power zone is a fast ball between the eyes."

Power had average speed, but succeeded in stealing home six times, including twice in the same game for the Indians in 1959. On the road, Power often visited museums and attended classical music concerts. He was the clubhouse practical joker, constantly needling teammates with his pranks. Power was traded to the Minnesota Twins for pitcher Pedro Ramos prior to the 1962 season.

Woodie Held
Shortstop, 1958–1964

Woodie Held was a shortstop with unusual power. He hit 29 home runs in his first season with Cleveland and added another 44 over the next two years. His best asset was his ability to play several positions, but his penchant for strikeouts led Cleveland to trade him to Washington after the 1964 season.

Jim Perry
Pitcher, 1959–1963; 1974–1975

Jim Perry pitched for the Indians in three different decades. In 1960, his second season in Cleveland, Perry, 23, had an outstanding year. He led the league with 18 wins and four shutouts. But when his victories began to slip, he was traded to Minnesota after the 1963 season.

In Minnesota, Perry had his best years. In 1965, he helped the Twins win the pennant. In 1969, he was a 20–game winner. In 1970, his 24 wins earned him the Cy Young award. Perry re–joined Cleveland in 1974 and pitched with his brother Gaylord for parts of two seasons. The Perrys are the second winningest brother combination in major league history, combining for 529 victories.

Jim "Mudcat" Grant
Pitcher, 1958–1964

Mudcat Grant was a consistent winner for the Indians. But despite winning 64 games in six years, Grant was traded to Minnesota early in 1964. The next year, he had a career year. Grant led the league with 21 wins and six shutouts, and helped the Twins capture the pennant by winning two games in the 1965 World Series. Cashing in on his sudden fame, he performed as a nightclub singer in the off–season. His group was called "Mudcat Grant and his Kitty Kats." After his playing days were over, Grant remained active in the Major League Baseball Alumni Association, raising money for retired ballplayers.

John Romano
Catcher, 1960–1964

Johnny Romano spent three seasons as the Indians' everyday catcher and was a two–time All–Star. His 25 home runs and 81 RBIs led the team in 1962. But in 1963, he was slowed by a fractured hand and his offense suffered. He was traded to the White Sox after the 1964 season.

John "Tito" Francona
Outfielder, 1959–1964

Tito Francona's best season in Cleveland was his first. Acquired from the Tigers for veteran Larry Doby, Francona hit .363 and belted 20 home runs in 1959. The following year, he led the league with 36 doubles, but his batting average began a steady decline. In 1965, Francona was traded to the Cardinals. He spent another five seasons in the majors, primarily as a pinch hitter. He retired after the 1970 season.

Gary Bell
Pitcher, 1958–1967

Gary Bell was a tall Texan with a blazing fastball. When he graduated from high school, he passed up numerous football and basketball scholarship offers to sign with the Indians for $4,000. He rose quickly through the system and arrived in Cleveland in 1958, where he won 12 games his first year. But Bell played for seven different managers in nine years and the constant change played havoc with his career. He found himself being shifted back and forth between the bullpen and the starting rotation. In 1966, he won a career–high 14 games and was promptly traded to Boston the following year.

Dick Donovan
Pitcher, 1962–1965

When Dick Donovan arrived in Cleveland in 1962, he was 34 and a veteran of 11 big-league seasons. He had won the league ERA title with Washington the year before, but was traded to the Indians for outfielder Jimmy Piersall. Donovan paid immediate dividends, winning 20 games for the Tribe. It was the high point of his career. Over the next three years, his game grew mediocre and in 1965, he retired.

Joe Azcue
Catcher, 1963–1969

Joe Azcue was the Indians' everyday catcher for two of his six seasons in Cleveland. He was behind the plate for Sonny Siebert's no–hitter in 1966, but his best season was 1968, when he batted .280 and was named to the All–Star team. Azcue was traded to the Red Sox early in 1969. In 1970, with the California Angels, he caught a second no–hitter.

Max Alvis
Third baseman, 1962–1969

Max Alvis spent six years as the Indians' everyday third baseman. While he never hit for a high average, Alvis was a regular run producer and hit more than 20 home runs in three different years. Alvis was considered an excellent fielder, but the arrival of Craig Nettles set the stage for his trade to Milwaukee after the 1969 season. He later retired to his native Texas and ran the bank in his hometown.

Tommy John
Pitcher, 1963–1964

Tommy John debuted in Cleveland at age 20 and Indians pitching coach Mel Harder considered him a budding star. But after he went 2–9 in 1964, John was included in the trade with the White Sox that brought Rocky Colavito back to Cleveland.

Harder turned out to be right about John. The tall lefthander became one of the most durable starters in the majors. During his 26–year career, John won 288 games, including three seasons as a 20–game winner.

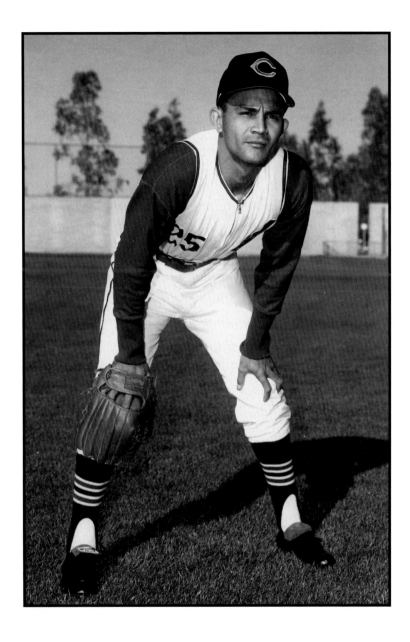

Vic Davalillo
Outfielder, 1963–1968

Vic Davalillo, a strong–armed center fielder, spent six years with Cleveland. In 1964, he won a gold glove. And in 1965, when he batted .301, he was named to the All–Star team. The diminutive Venezulean was traded to the Angels in 1968 and spent the next 10 years in the majors as a pinch hitter. He played in four World Series for three different teams.

Larry Brown
Infielder, 1963–1971

It was Larry Brown's glove, not his bat, that kept him in the Cleveland lineup. He was a superb defensive shortstop. In 1966, Brown was involved in an onfield collision at Yankee Stadium. While chasing a fly ball, he ran into teammate Leon Wagner, who was also racing for the ball. Brown suffered a broken nose and a fractured skull and was out for six weeks. In 1971, Brown was traded to Oakland.

Sam McDowell
Pitcher, 1961–1971

For six years, Sam McDowell was the dominant pitcher in the American League.

Cleveland signed McDowell out of high school and rushed the teenage pitching phenom to the major leagues at age 18. In his first start for the Indians in 1961, McDowell had a shutout going in the seventh inning, but threw so hard he fractured two ribs. Routinely, McDowell was so nervous on the days he pitched that he suffered stomach cramps and refused to talk to anyone, claiming, "I only pitch my best out of fear. I just have to get scared to pitch good. For me, pitching can never be great fun."

By 1964, after several demotions to the minors, McDowell made the majors for good. His overpowering fastball had the media comparing him to Sandy Koufax. But the pressure to live up to the hype caused McDowell to start drinking. He later recalled, "Baseball is the greatest and worst thing that ever happened to me. As it turned out, my talent was a curse. The curse was the way I handled it and didn't handle it. I was the biggest, most hopeless, and most violent drunk in baseball."

In 1965, McDowell finally harnessed his potential. He won 17 games, led the league in ERA and struck out 325 batters. Over the next five seasons, he led the league in strike-outs four times. But his teammates gave him little run support. In 1968, McDowell went 15–14, despite having the league's second lowest ERA at 1.81. In six of his starts, the Indians never scored a single run and nine of his losses were by one run. Contributing to McDowell's lack of wins was his insistence on throwing pitches other than his fastball. The Indians coaching staff wanted him to just blow hitters away. McDowell was stubborn, stating, "It's not fun throwing fastballs to guys who can't hit them. The real challenge is getting them out on stuff they can hit."

In 1970, McDowell reached the 20-win mark. The next season, he demanded a raise to $100,000. The Indians countered with an incentive-laden contract, the first of its kind, worth $92,000, but Commissioner Bowie Kuhn voided the contract, ruling the use of incentives illegal. McDowell was furious. He quit the team and demanded to be declared a free agent. He was suspended, and after he returned, his numbers took a steep dive. The Indians traded McDowell to the Giants for Gaylord Perry after the 1971 season. He played his final season with Pittsburgh in 1975.

In retirement, McDowell became a substance abuse counselor, working with ball players in the major and minor leagues.

Jack Kralick
Pitcher, 1963–1967

Jack Kralick had already thrown a no-hitter when he was traded by the Minnesota Twins to the Indians for pitcher Jim Perry. The tall, thin lefthander was known for his excellent control. His first year in Cleveland, Kralick went 13–9 for the Tribe. He won another 12 games in 1964. A severe auto accident early in 1967 led to his premature retirement.

Rutherford "Chico" Salmon
Infielder, 1964–1968

Chico Salmon's versatility was his greatest asset. He could play almost any position except pitcher or catcher, and he was the Tribe's premier pinch hitter. But Salmon may be best remembered for being superstitious. He believed in ghosts and slept with the lights on to ward off evil spirits. After the 1968 season, Salmon was traded to Baltimore, where he played in two World Series.

Leon "Daddy Wags" Wagner
Outfielder, 1964–1968

Leon Wagner was a power hitter who twice led the Indians in home runs. Already 30 years old when he arrived in Cleveland, Wagner was traded by the Los Angeles Angels after three seasons of hitting 25–plus home runs. While in Los Angeles, Wagner had appeared in several television series, including "The Man from U.N.C.L.E." He took his nickname from the slogan for his men's clothing store: "Buy your rags at Daddy Wags."

Wagner's first year with the Indians was his best. He hit 31 home runs and added 100 RBIs. By 1967, the Indians had a new manager, Joe Adcock, who insisted on platooning Wagner and Rocky Colavito in the outfield. Playing less meant a drop in Wagner's stats, and he was traded to the White Sox midway through the 1968 season.

Wilfred "Sonny" Siebert
Pitcher, 1964–1969

Sonny Siebert was signed by Cleveland after he led the University of Missouri baseball team to a second–place finish in the 1958 College World Series. A first baseman in college, Siebert became a pitcher in the minors. When he developed a devastating curveball, Siebert became a consistent winner for the Tribe. He twice won 16 games, and in 1966, he threw a no–hitter against Washington at Municipal Stadium. His next two years were marred by injuries and in 1969, Siebert was traded to the Red Sox for slugger Ken Harrelson. He spent another six years in the majors before retiring after the 1975 season.

Luis Tiant, Jr.
Pitcher, 1964–1969

Luis Tiant was the son of a great Cuban pitcher who pitched in the Negro Leagues before the color barrier was broken in 1947.

The Indians brought young Tiant to the majors in 1964. In his first start, he shut out the Yankees on four hits. He won 10 games in the season's final three months and his colorful personality was an instant hit. Tiant insisted on smoking cigars after every start. He even smoked them in the shower, where they somehow remained lit.

Tiant's big breakthrough came in 1968, when he changed his pitching delivery by turning his back to the hitter during his windup. The result was a 21–9 record. Tiant led the league with nine shutouts and a 1.60 ERA. The high point of the season came in June, when Tiant struck out 19 Minnesota Twins in a 10–inning game. His streak of 41 scoreless innings in 1968 set a club record that still stands. After the season ended, the Indians asked Tiant not to pitch winter ball, something he did every year. The request turned out to be a mistake. Tiant lost his control and in 1969, he lost 20 games and led the league in walks. Thinking he was through, Cleveland traded him to Minnesota.

Tiant won his first six starts for the Twins, but a shoulder injury cut short his season. Released by Minnesota, Tiant returned to the minors to regain his form. In 1972, he returned to the majors with Boston, where he won 15 games and was named the Comeback Player of the Year. Tiant was a 20–game winner for Boston three times in the next four years and won two games in the 1975 World Series against the Reds. His final season was with the Angels in 1982. He retired with 229 career victories.

Rocky Colavito
Municipal Stadium, 1965

After leaving Cleveland in 1959, Rocky Colavito hit 173 home runs and 532 RBIs in five years with Detroit and Kansas City. In 1965, the Indians brought him back and attendance soared to numbers not seen since he was traded.

Colavito didn't disappoint the faithful. His first year back, he hit 26 home runs and led the league with 108 RBIs. He played flawlessly in the field and completed all 162 games without a single error. In 1966, he added another 30 homers. But it was his last big year.

In 1967, Colavito voiced displeasure at being used as a part–time player and was traded mid–season to the White Sox. The following year, 1968, was his last season in the majors. Colavito retired with 374 career home runs. He later coached with Kansas City and the Indians.

Lou Piniella
Outfielder, 1968

Lou Piniella appeared in just six games for the Indians. Left unprotected in the expansion draft, Piniella ended up in Kansas City, where he was named 1969 American League Rookie of the Year. Traded to the Yankees five years later, Piniella's fiery attitude and hard–nosed play made him a fan favorite. After 11 years with the Yankees, he retired in 1984 to begin a career as a major league manager. Piniella managed the Yankees from 1986 to 1988 and the Cincinnati Reds from 1990 to 1992. In Cincinnati, he led the Reds to a four–game sweep of the favored Oakland A's in the 1990 World Series. In 1993, he took over as manager of the Seattle Mariners.

Ken "Hawk" Harrelson
Outfielder, 1969–1971

Ken Harrelson was nicknamed "Hawk" because of a prominent facial feature, but he was branded baseball's original "wild child" because of his long hair and outlandish wardrobe. Harrelson was a brash self–promoter, but a consistent run producer. He came to Cleveland from Boston early in 1969 after hitting 35 home runs and leading the league with 109 RBIs. He had another superb season his first year in Cleveland, with 30 home runs and 102 RBIs. Indians fans hadn't seen a power hitter like Harrelson since the departure of Rocky Colavito.

But in 1970, the excitement ended. Harrelson broke his leg sliding into second base during spring training and was sidelined until September. When he returned, his batting average plummeted and his power was gone. He played in just 69 more games for the Indians. In June of 1971, Harrelson suddenly quit baseball to try his luck as a professional golfer. He later worked as the White Sox' broadcaster and briefly, in 1986, as the team's general manager.

**Steve Hargan, "Sonny" Siebert, Sam McDowell, Luis Tiant
Starting rotation, 1968**

In 1968, for the second year in a row, the Indians pitchers led the American League in strike–outs. They also led the league with 23 shutouts and a combined 2.66 ERA. As a group, they stand alone in baseball history for having more strike–outs than hits–allowed. Nevertheless, their effort was good for only 86 wins and third place.

Vada Pinson
Outfielder, 1970–1971

Vada Pinson's best years were behind him by the time he arrived in Cleveland. The speedy outfielder twice had led the National League in hits and doubles in Cincinnati. But he broke his leg while playing for St. Louis, and the Cardinals traded him to Cleveland after one year. His first year with the Tribe, Pinson hit 24 home runs. But his run production fell dramatically in 1971 and the Indians traded him to the Angels. Pinson later spent 16 years as a major league coach with four different teams. He died of a stroke in 1995 at age 57.

Graig Nettles
Third baseman, 1970–1972

Graig Nettles was a part-time player with Minnesota before being traded to the Indians in a multi-player deal that sent Luis Tiant and Stan Williams to the Twins. Given a chance to play everyday, Nettles proved an offensive star. In his first two seasons, he led the team in home runs. His defensive prowess at third was even better. In 1971, Nettles set major league records for assists and double-plays by a third baseman in a single season. In one of the worst trades in Indians history, he was traded to the Yankees after the 1972 season for four players who never produced for Cleveland. He later played in five World Series with the Yankees and Padres, finishing his career with 390 home runs.

Ray Fosse
Catcher, 1967–1972; 1976–1977

The Indians selected Ray Fosse ahead of Johnny Bench with their first–round pick in the first free–agent draft in 1965. Fosse had unusually large hands and by 1970, was the Indians' everyday catcher. He played tough, and injured. He is best remembered for a bruising play in the 12th inning of the 1970 All–Star game, when the Red's Pete Rose was trying to score the winning run. Fosse blocked the plate but Rose bowled him over and broke the 4–4 tie for the National League. Fosse played the remainder of the season, hitting .307 with 18 home runs and winning the first of two consecutive Gold Glove awards. Only at season's end did Fosse discover that he had fractured his shoulder in the collision with Rose.

Nicknamed "Mule" for his ability to play through injuries, Fosse's offensive numbers declined sharply over the next three seasons. He was traded to Oakland after the 1972 season, where he went to three straight World Series. Fosse later returned to Cleveland for parts of two seasons, but injuries took their toll. He retired after the 1979 season and became a broadcaster and executive with the Oakland A's.

Gaylord Perry
Pitcher, 1972–1975

Hall of Fame pitcher Gaylord Perry had three of his best seasons while pitching for the Indians. Traded to Cleveland by the Giants after the 1971 season, Perry won 24 games for the fifth–place Indians in 1972 and was named the Cy Young award winner. He was the first pitcher to win the award in both leagues. Perry won 19 games in 1973 and 21 in 1974. He was often accused of throwing a spitball, and kept hitters and umpires guessing with his constant wiping of his hand on his cap and jersey.

In 1975, when Perry started slowly, he was dealt to the Texas Rangers for three players and $100,000 in cash. Two years later, he was traded to San Diego and went 21–6 in 1978 to win his second Cy Young award. He retired after the 1983 season with 314 victories. Perry was elected to the Hall of Fame in 1991.

Chris Chambliss
First baseman, 1971–1974

Cleveland signed Chris Chambliss in 1970 and sent him to Wichita, where he became the first player to win a AAA batting title in his first year. The next year, Chambliss was playing in Cleveland, where he became the American League Rookie of the Year. His batting average led the Indians for two years and in 1973, his 30 doubles were second best in the league. But the Indians were desperate for pitching help, and in 1974, Chambliss was traded to the Yankees for four pitchers who would go a combined 43–50 in their Cleveland careers. It was another case of Indians management trading quality for quantity. It was a pattern that would haunt Indians fans for the next two decades.

Dick Bosman
Pitcher, 1973–1975

Dick Bosman won only eight games for the Indians, but one will last for the ages.

In 1974, Bosman no–hit the Oakland A's before a crowd of 24,302 at Municipal Stadium. He threw just 89 pitches, but lost a perfect game when his own error gave the A's their only baserunner. Traded to Oakland in 1975, he won 11 games and helped the A's to the World Series. He later became a pitching coach with the White Sox, Orioles and Rangers.

Oscar Gamble
Designated hitter/outfielder,
1973–1975

Originally signed by scout
"Buck" O'Neill of the Cubs,
Oscar Gamble didn't become a
regular until traded to
Cleveland. He became the
club's designated hitter and hit
20 home runs in his first
season. Whenever Gamble
stepped to the plate, the
organist at Municipal Stadium
liked to play the theme from
"The Mickey Mouse Club"
because of how his cap looked
pulled down over his Afro.
Gamble was traded after the
1975 season to the Yankees,
where the management forced
him to cut his Afro. Frequently
traded, Gamble spent another
nine seasons in the majors.

Buddy Bell
Third baseman, 1972–1978

David Gus Bell was an outstanding defensive third baseman who won six consecutive Gold Glove awards after leaving Cleveland.

Bell took over for Graig Nettles at third base in 1973. He didn't possess the slugging power of former major league outfielder Gus Bell, his father, but his dazzling defense consistently ranked him among the league leaders in key defensive categories. His best offensive years came after his trade to Texas in 1978. He later played for the Reds and Astros before retiring after the 1989 season with 2,514 career hits. Bell later returned to the majors as a manager with the Tigers and Rockies.

George Hendrick
Outfielder, 1973–1976

George Hendrick was nicknamed "Silent George" for his refusal to talk to the press. He spoke with his bat and became one of the Indian's most consistent run producers. Drafted in 1968 in the first round by the Oakland A's, Hendrick was traded to Cleveland for catcher Ray Fosse. In his four seasons with the Tribe, he hit 89 home runs and was named to two consecutive All–Star teams.

John "Boog" Powell
First baseman, 1975–1976

After 14 seasons, Boog Powell was nearing the end of his career when he was traded to the Indians in 1975. During the previous 14 years in Baltimore, he had played in four World Series and been named league MVP in 1970. Powell had one last productive season for Cleveland in 1975, clubbing 27 home runs and driving in 86 runs. When he hit just nine home runs the next year, Powell was released.

Rico Carty
Designated hitter, 1974–1977

Nicknamed "The Big Boy" for his size, Rico Carty was a pure natural hitter who was plagued by injuries. He separated a shoulder three times and missed two entire seasons because of tuberculosis and a broken knee cap. Despite his injuries, Carty won the National League batting title in 1970 with the Braves, batting .366. When the Indians signed him mid–season in 1974, he was playing in the Mexican League. In Cleveland, Carty was openly critical of manager Frank Robinson and the feud between the two led to Carty being traded after the 1977 season. Carty retired after the 1979 season.

Jim Kern
Pitcher, 1974–1978; 1986

Jim Kern had a blazing fastball and a flaky personality. Early in his career, Kern's pitching was plagued by wildness. When he finally developed control, he became one of the league's most dependable relief pitchers. In the clubhouse, Kern delighted in pulling pranks on his teammates and reporters. Kern was traded to Texas for Bobby Bonds and Len Barker after the 1978 season. There he had 29 saves in 1979 before an elbow injury derailed his career. Kern pitched sparingly for five different teams over his final five seasons in the majors, and finished up with a return to the Indians in 1986, then retired.

Dennis Eckersley
Pitcher, 1975–1977

Dennis Eckersley joined Cleveland as a brash 20–year–old flamethrower. In 1975, he won 13 games and was named *The Sporting News* Rookie of the Year. In 1976, Eckersley, pitching both as a starter and a reliever, struck out 200 batters. His finest moment for Cleveland came in 1977 when he threw a no–hitter against the Angels at Municipal Stadium. It was part of a 22–inning hitless streak that just missed Cy Young's major league record of 23 innings, set in 1904. Eckersley made headlines for his shoulder–length hair and marital problems. His first wife, Denise, left him for teammate Rick Manning.

Eckersley was traded to the Red Sox after the 1977 season. In 1978, he won 20 games for Boston, and began to drink heavily. His career sputtered and he was traded to Oakland in 1987. Finally sober, he was returned to the bullpen, where he emerged as the dominant closer in the American League. His sidearm delivery helped lead the Athletics to three consecutive World Series appearances.

Frank Robinson
New York City, 1971

Frank Robinson was playing outfield for the Baltimore Orioles in 1971 when a New York newspaper published a report that said he would be named to manage the Indians, becoming the first black manager in major league history. There was just one problem. The report was premature. It would be another three years before Robinson would join the Indians, and 1975 before he was named manager, finally proving the earlier prediction correct.

Frank Robinson
Opening Day, 1975

Cleveland picked up Robinson off waivers late in the 1974 season and made him the designated hitter. Before the 1975 season started, he was named player/manager. On opening day, Robinson hit a home run in his first at bat and Cleveland beat the Yankees before 56,715 wildly excited fans at Municipal Stadium. In 1976, the Indians had their first winning season in eight years. But after getting off to a slow start in 1977, Robinson was fired after 57 games. He later managed the Giants and Orioles.

Rick Manning
Outfielder, 1975–1984

Rick Manning was a speedy outfielder known for making sensational defensive plays. He won a Gold Glove in 1976. Never a power hitter, he led the Indians in stolen bases three times. Manning was a fan favorite for his hustling style. He was traded to the Brewers for Gorman Thomas midway through the 1983 season, and soon became a part-time player. After retiring in 1987, Manning returned to Cleveland in 1990 and began broadcasting Indians games on television.

Bobby Bonds
Outfielder, 1979

Bobby Bonds had five seasons as a 30–30 player, hitting 30 home runs and stealing 30 bases. After spending his first seven years in the shadow of Willie Mays with the Giants, Bonds became a nomad, spending the next seven seasons playing for seven different teams. Cleveland acquired Bonds from the Texas Rangers, along with pitcher Len Barker, in one of the Indians' few successful trades. Bonds put up big numbers for the Tribe, hitting 25 home runs, driving in 85 RBIs and stealing 34 bases. When he asked that his contract be re–negotiated, Cleveland traded Bonds to the Cardinals. He later returned to Cleveland for four seasons as a coach/hitting instructor.

Andre Thornton
First baseman/designated hitter, 1977–1987

Andre Thornton came to Cleveland in one of the most lopsided trades in Indians' history. Cleveland general manager Phil Seghi sent pitcher Jackie Brown to Montreal for Thornton. In exchange for a pitcher who won just 10 games, the Indians got a slugger who anchored the team's offense for the next 10 years. Thornton hit more than 30 home runs in three seasons and twice drove in more than 100 runs. He was the best player on a team that posted only three winning seasons during his 10 years in Cleveland.

Thornton's career was plagued by injuries and tragedy. He spent almost two full seasons on the disabled list with bad knees and a broken thumb. In 1978, his van skidded off an icy highway and his wife and young daughter were killed. Through the adversity, Thornton remained a devoutly religious man. He didn't smoke, drink or use profanity. When his knees got bad enough, Thornton became the team's designated hitter. Injuries kept him from becoming the team's career home run leader. When he retired after the 1987 season, his 214 home runs ranked second behind Earl Averill's then team record of 226.

In high school, Rick Waits once threw back–to–back no–hitters. Signed by the Texas Rangers, Waits spent six years in the minors before becoming one of three players traded to Cleveland for Gaylord Perry. In 1980, Waits became the first Indians pitcher since Bob Feller to win on consecutive opening days. His best pitch was a curveball and his best season was 1979, when he won 16 games and threw three shutouts. Recurring knee problems shortened his career and he retired after the 1984 season.

Wayne Garland
Pitcher, 1977–1981

Even Wayne Garland had a hard time believing the Indians' offer. It came in 1976, when he was in the last year of a contract with Baltimore that paid $19,000 a year. In his first three years with Baltimore, Garland had won only seven games. But when he suddenly won 20 games and became a free agent, the Indians were eager to sign him. The club's new ownership, headed by Ted Bonda, wanted to send a message to the team's long suffering fans that they planned to build a winner. They offered Garland a 10–year, guaranteed contract for $2.3 million. Garland and his agent were dumbfounded. "Nobody gets a 10–year deal, and nobody's worth $2.3 million, certainly not me," Garland said. He told his agent, "Quick. Gimme a pen before they change their mind." Garland injured his arm in his first spring training appearance. He pitched the entire season with shoulder pain and won 13 games. Doctors later discovered that he had torn his rotator cuff. He continued to pitch, but was never the same again. After 15 wins over four seasons, Garland retired in 1981.

Baudilio "Bo" Diaz
Catcher, 1978–1981

Bo Diaz spent four seasons with Cleveland, sharing catching duties with Ron Hassey. Diaz was nicknamed "The Cannon" for his strong throwing arm, but weak hitting kept him from becoming a regular. Traded to Philadelphia after the 1981 season, he played for the Phillies and the Reds for another eight years. In 1990, Diaz was killed in a freak accident in his native Venezuela. He was on the roof of his home, adjusting a satellite dish, when the dish fell on him and crushed his skull. Bo Diaz died at 37.

Ron Hassey
Catcher, 1978–1984

Ron Hassey was an All–American at Arizona and a member of the 1976 NCAA baseball championship team. During his 13 years in the majors, Hassey was an everyday player for only four seasons, all of them in Cleveland. A good hitter, he was frequently used as a pinch hitter. Hassey was behind the plate for Len Barker's perfect game in 1981 and is the only catcher in major league history to catch two perfect games. Traded to the Cubs in 1984, he later played for the Yankees and the White Sox before going to three straight World Series with the Oakland A's.

Len Barker
Pitcher, 1979–1983

Len Barker was known for a blazing fastball, but it was his curveball that helped him make major league history. On May 15, 1981, before a crowd of 7,290 fans at Municipal Stadium, Barker pitched a perfect game against the Toronto Blue Jays. He threw just 103 pitches and struck out 11 batters by relying on his curveball almost exclusively after the third inning. Despite pitching on a cold rainy night, Barker had exceptional control. He recalled, "I knew I had good stuff, maybe awesome stuff. I had total command. I could throw anything anywhere I wanted."

Barker's 92–year old grandmother didn't fully grasp her grandson's accomplishment. She said, "Tell Len I'm proud. I hope he does better next time."

Barker twice led the league in strike–outs. His 15 wins for the Indians in 1982 was his last successful season. He was traded to the Braves late in 1983 for outfielder Brett Butler and third baseman Brook Jacoby.

Mike Hargrove
First baseman, 1979–1985

Drafted by Texas in the 25th round, Mike Hargrove became the American
League's Rookie of the Year in 1974. Hargrove used to drive fans and foes
to distraction with his elaborate rituals while in the batters' box, making
adjustments to his equipment after every pitch. It earned him the
nickname: "the human rain delay." But Hargrove had a discerning eye and
twice led the league in walks. He retired as a player after the 1986 season
and spent several years managing in the Indian's minor league system. In
1991, he was named manager of the Indians.

Colbert "Toby" Harrah
Third baseman, 1979–1983

Toby Harrah was traded to the Indians for the popular third baseman
Buddy Bell. Harrah had always played shortstop, but was moved to third
base by the Indians. Fans were tough on Harrah, who put up better
offensive numbers than Bell, but couldn't duplicate the acrobatic
defensive plays. Harrah provided a steady source of offense, leading the
Tribe in runs scored for four consecutive years. His best season in
Cleveland was in 1982, when he hit 25 home runs and drove in 78 runs.
He was traded to the Yankees after the 1983 season.

Joe Charboneau
Outfielder, 1980–1982

For one brief moment, no star shone brighter than that of Joe Charboneau. He hit a home run in his first game, led the team in home runs (23) and RBIs (87) in his first year, and was named the 1980 American League Rookie of the Year. He captivated Cleveland fans like no player since Rocky Colavito. The media nicknamed him "Super Joe" and a song about him became a hit on Cleveland area radio stations.

Charboneau was known as a tough guy. As a teenager, he used to box bare–knuckled for prize money. Once, in the minors, when he awoke from a drinking binge with a tattoo he didn't remember getting, he removed it himself with a razor blade. He won bets with teammates by swallowing lit cigarettes and whole raw eggs. He taught himself to open beer bottles with his eye socket and once performed a root canal on himself with a pair of pliers. (He said he couldn't afford the $400 dentist's fee.) His nose was broken six times, and because he had lost so much cartilage, he could drink beer through his nose with a straw.

Charboneau's playing career was cut short by two operations to remove two bulging discs from his spine. Sent to the minors, Charboneau never regained his prior form. When questioned by reporters, he remained upbeat about his brief moment of stardom. "The thought that my life is tragic, well, is ridiculous. Tragic is when somebody dies. When children are hungry, that's tragedy." By 1984, after a final season in the low minors, Charboneau's career was finally over. He was 28.

Rik "Bert" Blyleven
Pitcher, 1981–1985

Bert Blyleven was the premier curve ball pitcher of his era. By the time he arrived in Cleveland, he had already won 143 major league games. Early on with the Indians, elbow surgery cost him parts of two seasons, but he rebounded to win 19 games for the Tribe in 1984.

Blyleven was an habitual practical joker. During 1982 spring training in Arizona, he "mooned" radio sportscaster Pete Franklin during a live broadcast from the hotel lobby. It was the only time the outspoken Franklin was left speechless. Blyleven was also known for his shaving–cream pies and, once, he threw the Indians public relations man into a hotel swimming pool, fully clothed.

But on the mound, Blyleven was all business. He threw a no–hitter for the Rangers in 1977, and had 60 career shutouts. He had six seasons with 200–plus strike outs and nine years with at least 15 wins. Despite pitching for poor teams most of his career, Blyleven retired with 287 career victories. He later worked as a broadcaster on Minnesota Twins games.

Von Hayes
Outfielder, 1981–1982

Von Hayes was a pencil–thin outfielder blessed with great speed. In his only full season with the Indians, Hayes hit 14 home runs, drove in 82 runs and stole 32 bases. His reward was a trade to the Phillies for five players, including a young Julio Franco. In Philadelphia, he was tagged "Mr. Five–for–One" and, except for leading the league with 46 doubles in 1986, never lived up to fan expectations.

Rick Sutcliffe
Pitcher, 1982–1984

Rick Sutcliffe, a first–round draft pick of the Dodgers, was named the 1979 National League Rookie of the Year after winning 17 games his first year. When he struggled the next season, he was sent to the bullpen. And when he won just five games over the next two seasons, he was traded to Cleveland. There he won 14 games and led the league with a 2.96 ERA. He followed that with 17 wins in 1983. In 1984, in the final year of his contract, Cleveland traded Sutcliffe to the Cubs rather than lose him to free agency. In Chicago, the big right–hander went 16–1 and helped propel the Cubs to the division title. He was the unanimous choice to win the 1984 National League Cy Young award. Sutcliffe became the workhorse of the Cubs staff and, in 1987, led the league with 18 wins despite playing for a last–place team.

Julio Franco
Shortstop 1983–1988
First baseman/DH 1996–1997

As a rookie, Julio Franco led the Indians in RBIs, but his talent with the bat was overshadowed by his lack of grace with the glove. Franco developed a reputation as a sloppy fielder and led American League shortstops in errors for two straight years (1984, 1985). Franco was a frequent target of criticism, but his talent as a hitter kept him in the Indians lineup.

Franco's unorthodox batting style became his trademark. Coiling the bat behind his ear, his knees nearly touching, Franco became one of the league's premier hitters at his position. His 90 RBIs in 1985 were the most for an Indians shortstop since Lou Boudreau hit 106 in 1948. He was also a threat on the basepaths, stealing more than 25 bases three different times for the Tribe.

Traded to the Texas Rangers after the 1988 season, Franco's career soared. He won the AL batting title in 1991 and was selected to three straight All–Star teams. After a year with the White Sox and another playing in Japan, Franco returned to the Indians for two final seasons as the designated hitter. He led the team with a .322 average in 1996. He retired after the 1997 season at age 39.

Chris Bando
Catcher, 1981–1988

Chris Bando, the younger brother of Oakland A's slugger Sal Bando, spent his nine years in the majors as a back–up catcher. Recurring injuries kept him from developing into an everyday player. He never hit for a high average and only once, did he hit more than five home runs in a season. It was his ability to throw out base stealers that kept him on the roster. And Indians knuckleball pitchers Phil Niekro and Tom Candiotti both wanted Bando behind the plate. During the 1988 season, Bando was traded to Detroit. He retired a year later.

Pat Tabler
Infielder/outfielder/DH, 1983–1988

Pat Tabler was a first–round pick of the Yankees, but he spent his best years with the Indians. Tabler was a lethal hitter with players in scoring position. He had a career batting average of over .500 when the bases were loaded. Tabler became the team's designated hitter in 1987, but his lack of home run power eventually got him traded to the Royals for pitcher Bud Black during the 1988 season.

Mel Hall
Outfielder, 1984–1988

Mel Hall was acquired in the same trade that brought Joe Carter to Cleveland from the Cubs, but Hall never became the slugger everyone hoped he would be. In his rookie season with the Cubs, Hall hit 17 home runs. Traded to the Indians midway through the 1984 season, Hall suffered a season–ending injury in a car accident early in the 1985 season. He rebounded to hit 18 home runs in each of the next two years for Cleveland, but after hitting just six home runs in 1988, he was traded to the Yankees. While with the Indians, Hall gained notoriety for his stylish home–run trot. He placed a batting glove in each of his rear pants' pockets with the fingers pointing out. Hall claimed he was waving good–bye to opposing players as he rounded the bases.

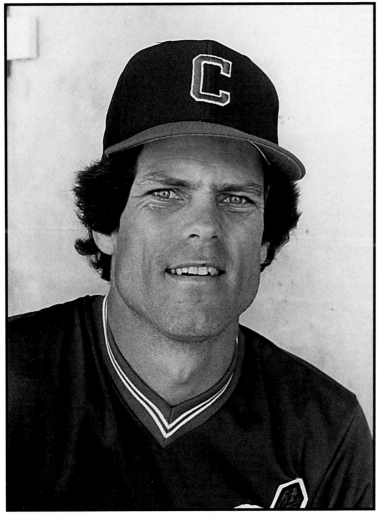

Brett Butler
Outfielder, 1984–1987

Brett Butler used his exceptional speed to steal bases and run down fly balls in the center–field expanse of Municipal Stadium. Butler came from the Braves, along with Brook Jacoby, in the famous trade for pitcher Len Barker. Butler was a pesky lead–off hitter everywhere he played and twice, he led the league in triples. In 1985, Butler became the first Indians player since Al Smith, in 1954–55, to score more than 100 runs in consecutive seasons. Butler was the major's best practitioner of the drag bunt. He signed as a free agent with the Giants for the 1988 season and later played with the Dodgers and Mets before retiring after the 1997 season with 558 career stolen bases.

Otis Nixon
Outfielder, 1984–1987

When it came to speed on the basepaths, Otis Nixon was the one.

Nixon stole 94 bases while playing for AAA Columbus, but the Yankees couldn't find a place for him and so they offered him to Cleveland. The Indians used Nixon as a pinch runner and a late–inning defensive replacement, but his weak bat prompted a trade to the Montreal Expos. The Expos let Nixon play everyday and once he was turned loose, he proved a late bloomer. Nixon stole 50 bases in 1990. After undergoing treatment for substance abuse, Nixon landed in Atlanta, where he stole 72 bases in 1991. At age 38 in 1997, his last season as an everyday player, Nixon stole 59 bases. Nixon started the 2000 season with 620 career stolen bases, ranking him 13th on the all–time list.

Brook Jacoby
Third baseman, 1984–1992

Brook Jacoby gave the Indians steady, if unspectacular, play at third base. A quiet player on and off the field, Jacoby was a two–time All-Star who had his best year in 1987, when he batted .300 and hit 32 home runs. Unfortunately, 27 of his home runs came with the bases empty. Jacoby had a superstitious habit of never washing the T–shirt he wore under his jersey, claiming the "strength" of the shirt aided his play. He retired after the 1992 season.

Joe Carter
Outfielder, 1984–1989

Joe Carter, was the second player taken in the 1981 draft after being named College Player of the Year by *The Sporting News*. He came to the Indians in 1984 in the deal that sent Rick Sutcliffe to the Cubs. Slowed by injuries early in his career, Carter had a break–out year in 1986. He led both leagues with 121 RBIs, the most by an Indians player in more than 30 years. His 200 hits in 1986 were the most since Al Rosen's 201 in 1953. And he was the first player in Indians history to have more than 20 homers, 20 stolen bases and 100 RBIs in a single season.

In 1987, Carter became the first 30–30 man in Indians history, hitting 32 home runs and stealing 31 bases. And with 106 RBIs, he became the first Indians player since Rocky Colavito to drive in more than 100 runs in consecutive years.

But all of Carter's offense in 1987 couldn't keep the woeful Indians from losing more than 100 games for the second time in three years. After another superb year in 1989, Carter was traded to San Diego for prospects Carlos Baerga and Sandy Alomar, Jr. Despite producing 115 RBIs for the Padres, Carter was traded again after just one year, this time to Toronto. He spent seven years with the Blue Jays and had the winning home run in Game 6 of the 1993 World Series. Carter retired after the 1998 season with 396 home runs and 10 seasons of 100–plus RBIs.

Phil Niekro
Pitcher, 1986–1987

Phil Niekro pitched in the major leagues until he was 48, surviving on a trademark knuckleball that helped him win 318 games. In April 1986, the Yankees waived Niekro and Cleveland picked him up. He won 11 games for the Tribe in 1986 and seven in 1987, before leaving to pitch his three final innings for his first team, the Atlanta Braves.

Niekro retired with 3,342 career strikeouts, good for eighth place on the all-time list. He and his brother, Joe, who spent 22 seasons pitching in the majors, won a combined 538 games, making the Niekro brothers the winningest brother combination in baseball history. In 1997, Phil Niekro was elected to the Hall of Fame.

Tom Candiotti
Pitcher, 1986–1991; 1999

Teammate Phil Niekro taught Tom Candiotti how to throw the knuckleball and the pitch changed his career. In the minors, Candiotti had never won more than 10 games in any of six seasons before he mastered the new pitch. With the Tribe in 1986, he won 16 games and led the league with 17 complete games. In 1987, he threw two one–hitters, but went 7–18 for the anemic Indians, who lost 101 games. Candiotti's best year in Cleveland came in 1988, when he went 14–8. He became the workhorse of the pitching staff and the first Indians pitcher since Sam McDowell to throw 200–plus innings for five straight years. Candiotti was traded to Toronto midway through the 1991 season and later spent six years with the Dodgers, before returning to Cleveland for one month in 1999.

Doug Jones
Pitcher, 1986–1991; 1998

Doug Jones spent nine years as a starting pitcher in the minor leagues and when he finally made it to the majors with Cleveland, he was made a reliever. Soon, he was one of the league's most dominant closers.

In 1988, Jones began a string of three seasons with at least 30 saves. His 43 saves in 1990 set a new club record, later eclipsed by Jose Mesa's 46 in 1995. The three–time All–Star had an off year in 1991 and went on to pitch for several teams before re–joining the Indians in July 1998, notching a single save.

Greg Swindell
Pitcher, 1986–1991; 1996

Greg Swindell was the second player taken in the 1986 draft and
before the year was out, he was pitching in the majors for Cleveland.
At the University of Texas, where he was a teammate of Roger
Clemens, Swindell set a slew of NCAA pitching records. In the minor
leagues, he pitched three games before the Tribe called him up in
August 1986. The big left-hander was a power pitcher. He possessed a
blazing fastball that struck out 97 batters in 102 innings his rookie
year. In 1987, Swindell's season was cut short by an elbow injury. He
returned in 1988 to win 18 games, including 12 complete games. But
in July 1989, when he was 13–2, a second elbow injury derailed his
season. A free agent after the 1991 season, Swindell returned to Texas
and spent four seasons with the Houston Astros, before rejoining the
Tribe late in the 1996 season. He spent the 1997 season with
Minnesota and later pitched for the Arizona Diamondbacks.

Cory Snyder
Outfielder, 1986–1990

Cory Snyder, the Indians' first–round draft pick in 1984, was a member of the 1984 U.S. Olympic baseball team and set numerous NCAA home run marks while playing at Brigham Young University. His strong arm and long blond hair were an instant attraction when he arrived in Cleveland in June 1986. Then, he hit 24 home runs in 102 games. Indians Manager Pat Corrales dubbed Snyder the "White Knight" and thought him the solution to the team's power drought. Despite Snyder's 33 home runs in 1987, the team finished in last place and Corrales was fired before season's end. Snyder's home runs came at a price: he led the team in strikeouts twice, including a club–record for right–handed batters, with 166 strike–outs in 1987. When his batting average and power numbers dropped for three straight years, Snyder was traded to the Chicago White Sox after the 1990 season. Over the next four seasons, he would play for four different teams before retiring after the 1994 season.

Dick Jacobs
Owner, 1986–1999

Dick Jacobs and his brother David purchased the Cleveland franchise in December 1986 for $35 million and started the team on the road to respectability. They invested in the farm system, added scouts and hired experienced baseball executives to run the day–to–day operations. It took six years but, finally, the infusion of cash and talent paid dividends. Building around a nucleus of talented draft picks, the franchise slowly improved just in time for the move to a new home.

Growing up in Akron, Jacobs knew all too well the downside of the aging Municipal Stadium. Plans were drawn up for a new ballpark and when Jacobs Field debuted in 1994, the team was a contender for the first time in more than 30 years. The team's on–field performance, combined with a gorgeous new facility, drew record crowds to Jacobs Field.

In 1999, after six sell–out seasons and record revenues, Jacobs sold the team to a local investors group headed by Larry Dolan for $323 million.

Albert Belle
Outfielder, 1989–1996

The only thing more frequent than Albert Belle's home run blasts was the talented outfielder's temperamental outbursts. Belle was kicked off his team at LSU in the middle of the 1987 College World Series, and the Indians suspended him several times in the minors for his tantrums. After several demotions to the minors, Belle finally became an everyday player in 1991, when he hit 28 home runs and drove in 95 RBIs. But Belle got the most headlines when he fired a ball into the stands at a heckler. The incident led to the first of numerous suspensions that Belle would serve.

Over the next three years, Belle put up huge power numbers, hitting 108 home runs and 342 RBIs. When he used a corked bat against the White Sox in 1994, suspicions were raised about his power. But Belle erased all doubts the next year when he hit 50 home runs, 52 doubles, batted .317 and drove in 126 runs. He became the first player to hit 50 doubles and 50 home runs in the same season. But Belle fumed again when he felt slighted by finishing second to Boston's Mo Vaughn in the balloting for the league's MVP award.

In 1996, Belle had another huge offensive season with 48 home runs and 148 RBIs. It would be his last for the Tribe. Belle signed with the White Sox once he became a free agent. He later played for the Orioles and while his "bad boy" reputation continued, he also remained one of the American League's premier run producers.

Carlos Baerga
Second baseman, 1990–1996; 1999

Very few players improve their stats dramatically after reaching the major leagues. Carlos Baerga is the exception.

Baerga produced mediocre offensive numbers in four minor–league seasons. He never hit more than 12 home runs. Never drove in more than 74 RBIs. And only once did he bat over .275. But after coming to the Indians with Sandy Alomar, Jr. in the trade for Joe Carter, Baerga became one of the league's premier offensive players.

In 1992, he batted .312, with 20 home runs and 105 RBIs. The next season was even better and he was voted to a second All–Star team. His back–to–back 200–hit seasons were the first by an Indians player since Dale Mitchell in 1948–49.

In 1993, Baerga, a switch hitter, became the first player to hit a home run from both sides of the plate in the same inning. His defensive skills helped solidify the Tribe's infield, and the arrival of shortstop Omar Vizquel in 1994 gave the Indians their best double–play combination in decades.

When his numbers slipped in 1996, Baerga was traded in late July to the New York Mets. He never recovered from the shock of leaving the Indians. His play declined sharply and he bounced around the majors and minors with several different organizations.

Sandy Alomar, Jr.
Catcher, 1990–

Since being named American League Rookie of the Year in 1990, Sandy Alomar's career has been plagued by injuries. In his first 10 seasons with Cleveland, he has caught more than 90 games only four times. When healthy, Alomar has provided superb defense behind the plate and shown a knack for getting timely hits. In 1997, free of injuries, Alomar had a career year. He hit .324 and belted 21 home runs. His 83 RBIs were the most ever by an Indians catcher. He had a 30–game hitting streak and was named the MVP of the All–Star game. His performance in the postseason was even better. His 19 RBIs were the most ever by a player in the postseason and his five home runs set a record for catchers in the postseason. But a series of knee operations kept Alomar from producing on a consistent basis and he played only 37 games in 1999.

Mike Hargrove
Manager, 1991–1999

For a franchise that had 36 managers in 100 years, Mike Hargrove brought stability and a winning attitude to the Indians. In his eight–plus seasons with the Tribe, the team won five Central Division titles, two American League pennants and twice went to the World Series. His 721 career victories ranked him second all–time behind Lou Boudreau's 728.

Originally the team's first base coach, Hargrove took over for John McNamara in July 1991. Considered a player's manager, he was popular with the players and fans. But the team's inability to win a World Series title ultimately cost him his job. Fired after winning 97 games in 1999, Hargrove was named manager of the Baltimore Orioles for the 2000 season.

Kenny Lofton
Outfielder, 1992–1996; 1998–

Every successful team needs an offensive
catalyst and Kenny Lofton is the
sparkplug that ignites the Indians'
high–voltage offense. Lofton is the
Indians' all–time leader in stolen bases,
and his ability to get on base makes him
one of the league's best "table–setters."
His 66 steals in 1992 led the league and
set a rookie record. A four–time Gold
Glove winner, Lofton excelled at
covering the vast center–field of Jacobs
Field. Lofton was traded to the Atlanta
Braves for Dave Justice and Marquis
Grissom just prior to the start of the
1997 season, but returned to the Indians
as a free agent in 1998. Injuries slowed
him down in 1999, when he failed to
steal 50 bases for only the second time in
his career.

Jim Thome
Infielder/designated hitter, 1991–

Jim Thome's tape–measure home runs and blue–collar work ethic make him a fan favorite in Cleveland. Originally a third baseman, Thome was moved to first base after the 1996 season to make room for Matt Williams. There, he developed into one of the American League's most lethal run producers, hitting more than 30 home runs for four straight years. In 1999, he became the first player since Mickey Mantle in 1958 to lead the league in walks and strike–outs in the same season. And his 171 strike–outs set a new Indians single–season record. Thome regularly saved his best for the postseason, hitting 16 home runs in 50 postseason games to rank third behind Reggie Jackson and Mickey Mantle, both of whom hit 18. His four home runs and 10 RBIs against Boston in the 1999 ALCS couldn't keep the Indians from falling to the Red Sox in five games.

Eddie Murray
Designated Hitter, 1994–1996

Eddie Murray was a model of consistency at the plate, driving in at least 75 runs for 19 consecutive seasons. A quiet man who avoided the press, he provided veteran leadership in the clubhouse. In 1996, Murray joined Hank Aaron and Willie Mays as the only three players in major league history to hit 500 home runs and get 3,000 career hits. His knack for producing big hits in key situations helped propel the 1995 Indians to the World Series, where his RBI–single in the 12th inning won Game 3.

Chad Ogea
Pitcher, 1994–1998

After pitching Louisiana State University to the College World Series title in 1991, Ogea was drafted by the Indians in the third round. But the big right–hander's career was beset by injuries and he never won more than 10 games in any of his four years with Cleveland. The high point of his career was the 1997 World Series, where he won two games and became the first Indians pitcher since Jim Bagby in 1920 to drive in a run in the World Series. Ogea was traded to the Phillies after the 1998 season.

Matt Williams
Third baseman, 1997

Although he spent just one season in Cleveland, Matt Williams put up the best offensive numbers by an Indians third baseman since Al Rosen four decades earlier. Williams hit 32 home runs and 105 RBIs after arriving from the San Francisco Giants, where he spent his first seven seasons. With the Giants, he had four seasons with 30-plus home runs and in 1990, he led the National League with 122 RBIs. Williams was traded to the Arizona Diamondbacks for Travis Fryman in a multi-player deal after the 1997 season.

Brian Giles
Outfielder, 1995–1998

After the 1998 season, the Indians brass deemed outfielder Brian Giles expendable and dealt him to the Pittsburgh Pirates for pitching help. It proved a costly miscalculation, as Giles proved to be a late bloomer. Given a chance to play everyday, he had a monster year for the Pirates in 1999, hitting 39 home runs, driving in 115 runs and batting .315.

Dennis Martinez
Pitcher, 1994–1996

Dennis Martinez is the winningest Latin American pitcher in baseball history. He was signed by Cleveland at age 38, after winning 208 games over 17 seasons with the Orioles and Expos. He produced 32 wins in three years with the Indians and his seven shutout innings against Seattle in Game 6 of the 1995 ALCS sent the Tribe to their first World Series in 31 years. A national hero in his native Nicaragua, "El Presidente" earned his final victory with the Atlanta Braves in 1998. His 245 career wins eclipsed the 243 won by Hall of Famer Juan Marichal, who had previously held the record for Latin American pitchers.

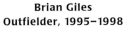

Paul Assenmacher
Pitcher, 1995–1999

In an age of specialization, pitcher Paul Assenmacher was Manager Mike Hargrove's left-handed ace in the hole. Used in late-inning situations, Assenmacher proved exceptionally reliable in holding leads for the Tribe. Unusually durable, he appeared in 14 of the Indians' 18 postseason games in 1997. At age 39, he was released after the 1999 season.

Orel Hershiser
Pitcher, 1995–1997

After 11 seasons with the Los Angeles Dodgers, Orel Hershiser was signed as a free agent by Cleveland in 1995. His first season for the Tribe was his best since 1988, when he won 23 games and the Cy Young award. He won 16 games and had a phenomenal postseason, winning four games and posting a 1.53 ERA. In 1996, Hershiser won another 15 games for the Indians and 14 more in 1997. He signed with San Francisco for the 1998 season, before briefly returning to the Dodgers.

Jose Mesa
Pitcher, 1992–1998

Originally a starting pitcher, Jose Mesa was made a reliever and became the anchor of the Indians bullpen for several seasons. In 1995, he set a team record with 46 saves and finished second to Seattle's Randy Johnson in the Cy Young balloting. With another 39 saves in 1996, Mesa was selected to his second straight All–Star team. However, Indians fans will always remember Mesa for his blown save in Game 7 of the 1997 World Series. With the Indians leading 2–1 in the ninth inning, Mesa's inability to close out the Florida Marlins cost the Tribe the championship.

Bartolo Colon
Pitcher, 1997–

Cleveland signed Bartolo Colon as an undrafted free agent out of the Dominican Republic. In 1998, Colon struck out 14 Toronto batters in a single game, threw six complete games and was named to the All–Star team. His complete–game victory over the Yankees in the 1998 ALCS made him the first Indians hurler to throw a complete game in the post–season since Bob Lemon in 1954. And in 1999, Colon became the first Indians pitcher to win 18 games since Greg Swindell in 1988.

Omar Vizquel
Shortstop, 1994–

In an era of exceptional American League shortstops, Omar Vizquel continues to amaze Indians fans with his acrobatic play. Acquired from Seattle after five seasons with the Mariners, Vizquel won a Gold Glove in his first season with Cleveland, becoming the first Indians shortstop in club history to be so honored. In 1999, he became the first AL shortstop to win seven consecutive Gold Glove awards. Exceptionally quick, he stole 35 or more bases for four straight years (1996–99) and teamed with outfielder Kenny Lofton to give the Tribe a terrific one–two offensive punch at the top of the batting order. Vizquel had a career offensive year in 1999, hitting .333 and scoring 112 runs.

Manny Ramirez
Outfielder, 1993–

Manny Ramirez, named 1991 High School Player of the Year in New York City, was the Indians' 1991 first-round draft pick. On a team that generates runs in bunches, Ramirez has become the Tribe's leading offensive weapon.

Ramirez's 165 RBIs in 1999 set a new team record and was the highest total in the majors in 60 years. By age 27, he hit 10 career grand-slams, the only player besides Jimmie Foxx to hit nine grand slams before the age of 27. Ramirez is the only player in Indians history to have consecutive seasons of 130-plus RBIs. A potential free agent after the 2000 season, Ramirez's future in Cleveland is the subject of considerable speculation, and sure to generate headlines regardless of the outcome.

David Justice
Outfielder, 1997–2000

David Justice was the 1990 National League Rookie of the Year with the Atlanta Braves. His home run in Game 6 of the 1995 World Series gave the Braves the only run they needed to defeat the Indians, 4–2. After missing almost the entire 1996 season with shoulder surgery, Justice was traded to Cleveland, along with Marquis Grissom, for outfielder Kenny Lofton just prior to the start of the 1997 season. His 33 home runs, 101 RBIs and .329 average for the Indians earned him the league's Comeback Player of the Year award in 1997. Despite 21 home runs and 57 RBIs by June 30, Justice was traded to the Yankees in 2000 for three prospects.

Charles Nagy
Pitcher, 1990–

During the 1990s, Charles Nagy has been the anchor of the Indians pitching staff. He has been the model of consistency, winning at least 15 games in six of his nine full seasons with the Tribe. A member of the 1988 Olympic team, Nagy was a first–round pick of the Indians. He has led the Indians staff in strikeouts five times and is a three–time All Star.

Dave Burba
Pitcher, 1998–

Before he arrived in Cleveland to help solidify the Indians starting rotation, Dave Burba had never won more than 11 games in any of his six major league seasons. But in each of his first two years with the Tribe, he threw 200–plus innings and won 15 games. It's been Burba's ability to eat up innings that has proved his greatest asset. In 1999, he had three games with 10 or more strike–outs and fanned 13 Toronto batters in July at Jacobs Field.

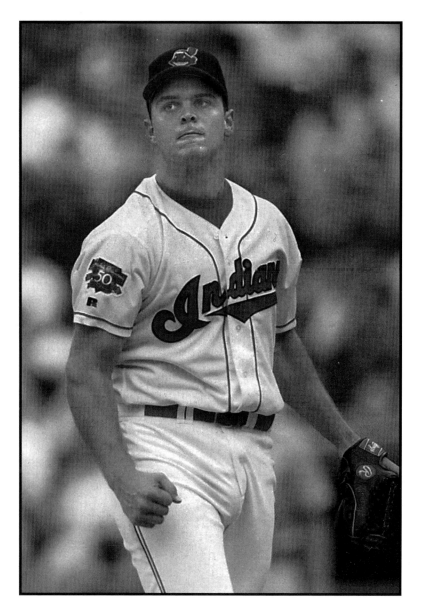

Jaret Wright
Pitcher, 1997–

The son of a former major league pitcher, Jaret Wright's blazing fastball got him to the majors at age 21. Called up to the Indians midway through the 1997 season, Wright went 8–3 to help pitch the Tribe into the playoffs. His two victories over the Yankees in the ALCS were followed up by a victory in Game 4 of the World Series over the Florida Marlins. But Wright's sudden success at an early age proved shortlived. Despite winning 12 games in 1998, Wright, a former first–round draft pick of the Indians, has struggled with injuries and inconsistency.

Richie Sexson
First baseman/designated hitter, 1997–2000

The Indians thought so much of prospect Richie Sexson that they traded Sean Casey to the Reds to make room for him. Sexson's ability to fill in for the injured Jim Thome at first during the stretch run in 1998 made him an instant fan favorite. Nicknamed "Big Bird" for his tall, slender build, Sexson earned a chance to play every day in 1999 and had a huge year. He hit 31 home runs, drove in 116 RBIs in 134 games and his seven triples led the team. Desperate for pitching help, Cleveland traded Sexson to Milwaukee in July 2000.

Travis Fryman
Third baseman, 1998–

Before coming to Cleveland in 1998, Travis Fryman spent seven seasons with the Detroit Tigers, where he hit 140 home runs, drove in 652 runs and was a four-time All-Star. Traded to the Arizona Diamondbacks after the 1997 season, Fryman was later sent to the Indians for third baseman Matt Williams. Fryman hit a career-high 28 home runs in 1998 for the Tribe and gave the Indians a steady presence at third base. Injuries limited him to just 85 games in 1999 and his .255 average was the lowest of his career.

Roberto Alomar
Second baseman, 1999–

An 11–time All–Star, Roberto Alomar has been the American League's premier second baseman since the early 1990s. The winner of eight Gold Glove awards, his dazzling defense has set a standard by which all others are judged. Signed as a free agent by Cleveland after playing eight seasons with the Blue Jays and Orioles, Alomar had the finest year of his career in 1999. He led the AL in runs scored with 138, the second–highest total in club history. Alomar batted .323 and added 24 home runs and 120 RBIs. His heady play in the field and unselfishness at the plate made him an instant favorite with Indians fans.

Mike Hargrove and John Hart
Jacobs Field, 1999

General manager since 1991, John Hart has directed the Indians' rebirth. He rebuilt the team with deft trades, overhauled the farm system and signed key free agents. He signed the team's younger players to long–term contracts, which proved a windfall on the field and at the gate.

Manager Mike Hargrove molded veterans and prospects into the American League's most feared offense. The team won five consecutive Central Division titles under Hargrove and went to two World Series. But a quick exit in the first round of the 1999 playoffs spelled the end for Hargrove. Despite all of the success, Hart fired Hargrove and replaced him with hitting coach Charlie Manuel for the 2000 season.

**Sandy and Roberto Alomar
Spring training, 1999**

Reunited for the first time in 10 years, the sons of former major leaguer Sandy Alomar, Sr., pose together in the dugout during spring training. The Alomar brothers played together for eight games in San Diego before Sandy was traded to the Indians in 1990. They are the first brothers to be named the MVP of an All–Star game, Sandy in 1998 and Roberto in 1999. Together they have been to 17 of the summer classics.

Photograph Index

Photograph Credits

Akron Beacon Journal:
25, 134 (left), 146, 165, 167, 168 (right), 171, 172, 173, 174 (right), 175, 176, 178, 180, 181, 182, 183, 184, 186, 187, 188, 189, 190, 191, 192 (left), 193, 194, 195, 196, 197, 198, 199, 200, 202, 203, 207

Blank, Steve:
20 (left), 56 (top)

Cincinnati Enquirer, The:
frontispiece, 12, 26, 32, 40, 42, 44, 52, 62, 76 (right), 136 (right)

Cleveland Plain Dealer:
19, 41, 47, 56 (bottom), 66, 71, 81 (left), 88 (left), 89, 92, 98, 105, 115, 130, 134 (right), 136 (left), 138 (right), 141, 142, 143, 145, 147, 150, 153, 154, 163, 164, 166 (right), 174 (left), 177, 179

Cleveland Public Library:
84, 86 (right), 90, 96, 101, 112, 121, 129 (left)

**Cleveland State University
(Cleveland Press Archives):**
51, 60, 67 (right), 69, 73, 74, 79, 80, 86 (left), 100 (left), 114, 116, 117 (left), 120, 123, 124, 125, 129 (right), 131, 132, 135, 137, 138 (left), 139, 144, 151, 155, 158, 159, 166 (left), 168 (left), 170

Goldstein, Dennis:
16, 18 (right), 21, 22, 23 (right), 24, 30, 31, 36, 38, 50, 54, 57 (right), 58, 63, 64, 77, 78 (right), 95, 100 (right), 103, 108, 113, 117 (right), 126

Kuntz, Ron:
185, 192 (right), 201

Loughman, Bill:
29 (right) ,45, 59, 65, 76 (left), 83, 97, 102, 104, 118, 122, 148, 149, 160

McWilliams, Doug:
152, 156, 157, 162

Mumby, Mike:
8, 10, 13, 17, 20 (right), 23 (left), 29 (left), 37, 39, 46, 61, 67 (left), 75, 87, 93

National Baseball Library:
15, 18 (left), 43, 53, 81 (right), 82, 106, 110, 119, 133, 140

Patterson, Ted:
55

SABR/Ottoson Files:
70, 72, 91

Stang, Mark:
34, 35, 48, 49, 85, 99, 109, 128

The Sporting News:
9, 14, 27, 28, 33, 57 (left), 68, 78 (left), 88 (right), 94, 107, 127, 161, 169

**Western Reserve Historical Society,
Cleveland, Ohio:**
11

**Jacobs Field
September 7, 1995**

Indians fans counted down the days until the Indians captured their first A.L. Central Division title. It would mean the team's first pennant in over 40 years and lead to a World Series against the Atlanta Braves. Baseball was finally back in Cleveland.

To order additional copies of *Indians Illustrated*, or for information about other titles
currently available from Orange Frazer Press, please call **1–800–852–9332**,
or visit our website at **orangefrazer.com**. Address inquiries to:
Orange Frazer Press
P.O. Box 214
37½ West Main Street
Wilmington, OH 45177.